Second Edition

IDITAROD
Fact Book

A Complete
Guide to
The Last
Great Race®

Edited by Tricia Brown

EPICENTER PRESS
Alaska Book Adventures™
WWW.EPICENTERPRESS.COM

Publisher: Kent Sturgis
Acquisitions Editor: Lael Morgan
Editor: Tricia Olson
Contributor: Andrea Bachhuber
Editorial Assistant: Jennifer Houdek
Cover & Text Design: Victoria Michael
Map: Marge Muehler, Gray Mouse Graphics
Proofreader & Indexer: Sherrill Carlson
Printer: Transcontinental Printing

Epicenter Press publishes books about art, history, nature, and diverse cultures and lifestyles of Alaska and the Pacific Northwest.

Trademark notice: The Iditarod Trail Committee holds registered trademarks for the following: Iditarod Trail Alaska, Alaska where men are men and women win the Iditarod, The Last Great Race, 1,049 miles, Anchorage to Nome, and Mushing the Iditarod Trail.

Library of Congress Control Number: 2006934262

ISBN 10: 0-9745014-9-2
ISBN 13: 978-0-9745014-9-9

To order a single copy of the IDITROD FACT BOOK, mail $14.95 plus $5.00 for shipping (WA residents add $1.60 for state sales tax) to Epicenter Press, PO Box 82368, Kenmore, WA 98028; call toll-free to 800-950-6663; or order online at www.EpicenterPress.com.

green press
INITIATIVE

The text pages for the first printing of 4,400 copies of this book were printed on 3,380 pounds of recycled, acid-free paper with 100% post-consumer content. According to the Green Press Initiative, use of this recycled paper made it possible to conserve 41 mature trees (averaging 40 feet tall and 6-8" in diameter), 14,788 gallons of water, 1,951 pounds of solid waste, the equivalent of 3,563 pounds of net green house gases, and 37 million BTUs of total energy. These calculations from Environmental Defense are based on information supplied by the Pulp & Paper Technology Program at the University of Maine. For more information, visit www.GreenPressInitiative.org.

First Edition October 2006
10 9 8 7 6 5 4 3 2 1
Printed in Canada

© 2006 Jeff Schultz / AlaskaStock.com

Dedicated to
SUSAN BUTCHER
1955 - 2006

an Iditarod champion,
a genuine Alaska hero,
a wife and mother,
and a woman of great strength
who never gave up

Rick Mackey readies his team at the 1983 starting line. That airborne wheel dog was named Jumper.

CONTENTS

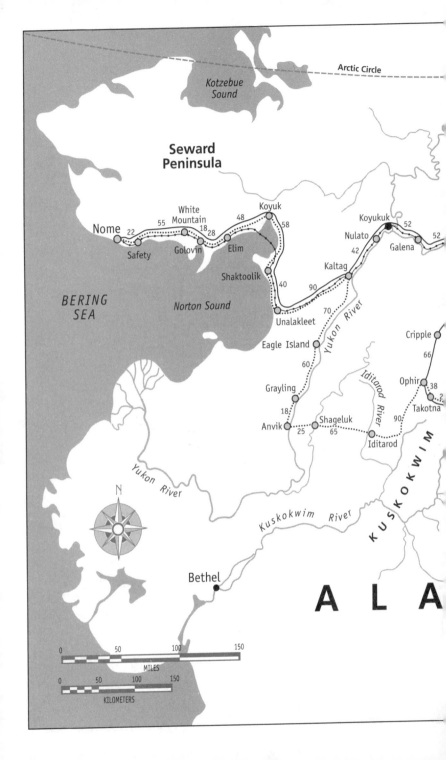

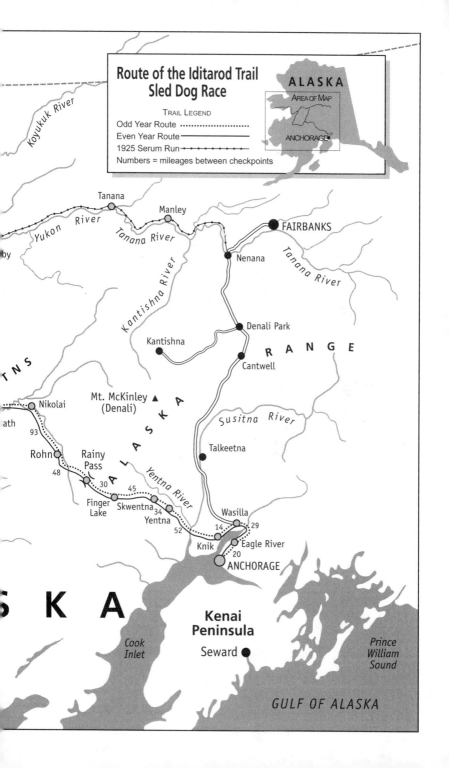

A Grand Idea

THE SERUM RUN

In February 1925—the depths of winter—the village of Nome, Alaska, had been exposed to diphtheria, and its children needed life-saving antitoxin serum. Mushers responded, and a tale of heroism ensued.

The story began when Dr. Curtis Welch diagnosed the diphtheria outbreak. Diphtheria is a serious contagious bacterial disease marked by high fever, weakness, and the formation in the throat and other air passages of false membranes that create breathing difficulties. For children, in particular, it can be fatal.

Dr. Welch sent telegraphed messages to Fairbanks, Anchorage, Seward, and Juneau, asking for help. The only serum available was in Anchorage at the Alaska Railroad Hospital, where Dr. John B. Beeson had 300,000 units. But Anchorage to Nome is more than 1,000 miles. And time was of the essence.

Despite the arguments of those who wanted to transport by air, Gov. Scott C. Bone rejected the idea as too dangerous. He decided the speediest, most reliable way to get the serum to Nome was via dogsled. He called on the Northern Commercial Co.—the largest organization in the Yukon River area—to arrange for relay teams. Men of the Army Signal Corps, at their scattered telegraph stations, also assisted in communicating with the mail carriers along the trail.

Nome musher and Siberian husky breeder Leonhard Seppala was instrumental in helping to save the lives of many people during a diphtheria outbreak in Nome, 1925. His leaders, Togo and Balto, gained national fame and he later toured the country with them.

From the Otto Nordling Collection, UAF 1974-135-1, Archives, Alaska and Polar Regions Collections, Rasmuson Library, University of Alaska Fairbanks

The serum was packed up in Anchorage in a cylinder. Dr. Beeson wrapped it in a quilt for insulation, then it was tied up in canvas for further protection from freezing. The first relay of the journey was by train from Anchorage to Nenana. The train arrived in Nenana on Tues., Jan. 27, 1925, at 11 p.m. Conductor Frank Knight gave the bundle to the first of twenty mushers, William "Wild Bill" Shannon, who took it on the first leg of the 674 miles to Nome. With Interior temperatures at a twenty-year low, Shannon left in –50° F cold. Mail carriers, most of them Native men, would carry the serum in the relay, with the plan to connect with Alaska Sweepstakes champion Leonhard Seppala at Nulato. His dogs were famous as the fastest in the territory.

When Seppala's turn approached, he left Nome, intending to rendezvous at Nulato and return with the serum. But near Shaktoolik, he came upon Henry Ivanoff, who shouted to Seppala, "The serum! The serum! I have it here!" Seppala accepted the package, then turned around and mushed toward Nome. He crossed the frozen Norton Sound with temperatures hovering at -30° F and a brutal wind chill of -85° F. The gale blew out the trail in the winter darkness, making it difficult for his lead dog Togo at the head of the team. Still, he made it to Golovin, 91 miles down the trail, after traveling a total of 260 miles, and passed the serum to Charlie Olson.

Togo was mounted and placed on display after his death. Visitors to the Iditarod Trail Committee Headquarters near Wasilla can see him in the Iditarod museum.

June Price

Finally, after 19 other mushers carried the serum, Gunnar Kaasen drove his tired dog team—led by another of Seppala's lead dogs, Balto—down an almost deserted First Avenue on Feb. 2, 1925. The serum had reached the town in an epic run. Dogs and men alike had suffered frostbite, and several dogs perished for the sake of human lives in Nome.

Today's Iditarod Trail Sled Dog Race honors the men and dogs of the 1925 serum run and follows some of the same trails they used more than eighty years ago. (Sources: www.iditarod.com and www.serumrun.org)

In 1997, famed arctic explorer and musher Col. Norman Vaughan organized the first running of an annual event that exactly retraces the 1925 serum run route. Titled the Norman Vaughan Serum Run 25, the event is less a race and more an educational expedition with two goals: to retell the stories of the 1925 mushers and dogs, and to educate villagers along the way about the importance of childhood inoculations. Double-teams of mushers/dogs and snowmachines journey west from Nenana to Nome through more than 750 miles of wilderness. The 2006 run began on Feb. 19 at Nenana, with the reenactment of serum delivery from an Alaska Railroad representative.

THE SERUM RUN MUSHERS OF 1925

MUSHER	LEG OF SERUM RUN	MILES
"Wild Bill" Shannon	Nenana to Tolovana	52
Edgar Kalland	to Manley Hot Springs	31
Dan Green	to Fish Lake	28
Johnny Folger	to Tanana	26
Sam Joseph	to Kallands	34
Titus Nikolai	to Nine Mile Cabin	24
Dave Corning	to Kokrines	30
Harry Pitka	to Ruby	30
Billy McCarty	to Whiskey Creek	28
Edgar Nollner	to Galena	24
George Nollner	to Bishop Mountain	18
Charlie Evans	to Nulato	30
Tommy Patson	to Kaltag	36
Jackscrew	to Old Woman	40
Victor Anagick	to Unalakleet	34
Myles Gonangnan	to Shaktoolik	40
Henry Ivanoff	to meeting with Seppala	
Leonhard Seppala*	to Golovin	91
Charlie Olson	to Bluff	25
Gunnar Kaasen	to Nome	53

Seppala set out from Nome, met Ivanoff outside of Shaktoolik, turned around, and carried the serum onward to Golovin, 91 miles away, traveling a total distance of 260 miles.

BIRTH OF THE LAST GREAT RACE

Mush dog teams a thousand miles across the Last Frontier? In 1973, some said it couldn't be done. But a core of believers, led by the man who became known as the Father of Iditarod, Joe Redington, Sr., knew that it could and set out to make it so.

The idea of a race along the historic Iditarod Trail had been talked about for years, at least in passing. In 1967, the 100th anniversary of Alaska's purchase from Russia, a Wasilla woman named Dorothy Page promoted the idea of holding a dog sled race as part of the celebration. The race was held on the old Iditarod Trail, but was just 28 miles long. Could dogs race more than 1,000 miles along that trail from Anchorage all the way to Nome? The one true believer always was Redington, a leathery-faced sourdough who came to Alaska from Oklahoma, founded a kennel in Knik, and devoted much of his life to mushing.

By 1973, Redington was ready to try out the race. Originally, he proposed a mush from Anchorage to Iditarod, the mining ghost town some 500 miles down the trail. Dick Mackey, then an Anchorage sprint musher, was one of the most enthused of those who listened to Redington and saw the possibilities for excitement in a long-distance event. "No one's heard of Iditarod. Why don't you run to Nome?" Done!

Redington worked with Tom Johnson and Gleo Huyck to incorporate the Iditarod, but when Redington guaranteed

The Iditarod National Historic Trail.
Bureau of Land Management

a purse of $50,000 at the finish line, he astounded the mushing community. At the time, said Howard Farley, also an initial organizer, there wasn't $50,000 in prize money for all the dog races in the world combined. But the promised purse became reality when old World War II Eskimo Scouts leader Col. "Muktuk" Marston donated $10,000 and the Bank of the North approved the cosigning of a $30,000 loan for Redington by local businessman Bruce Kendall. Redington put up his Knik home as collateral and the frantic fund-raising effort kept him from entering the race he created. (Source: *Iditarod Silver* / Epicenter Press)

MOVERS AND SHAKERS

While many people were instrumental in launching the now-famous Iditarod Trail Sled Dog Race, two individuals are today remembered as the "Father" and "Mother" of the Iditarod.

Joe Redington, Sr., portrait with lead dog 'Feets.'
© 2006 Bill Devine / AlaskaStock.com

Joe Redington, Sr.

Joe Redington, Sr., was born in Oklahoma on the Chisholm Trail and grew up during the Depression—homeless, motherless, roaming the country looking for work as a field hand. Alaska was his rebirth in 1948. Redington found the home he had never had. On his own piece of dirt, a man could raise a family, hunt, fish, run dogs and stand up for what he believed.

Redington, his wife, Vi, and their children homesteaded at Flat Horn Lake and in Knik. He had been a big-game guide, a Bush pilot, a miner, and a commercial fisherman, but above all he loved dog mushing. At its peak his kennel housed 500 huskies.

Almost single-handedly, Redington rescued Alaska dog mushing from extinction. Seeing dogs disappearing in villages across the state and the snowmachine appearing, he felt something had to be done. With ambition, his abiding love for sled dogs, and refusal to accept "it can't be done," Redington created a legacy in a thousand-mile race across Alaska, and earned the title, "Father of the Iditarod." Redington was named to the Iditarod Hall of Fame in 1997. He ran the race nineteen times—every year from 1974 to 1992. His best finish was 5th, in 1975, 1977, and 1978. His fastest time was in 1989 with 12 days, 2 hours, 57 minutes, 16 seconds. He was chosen Most Inspirational in 1988, 1989, and 1997, and received the Sportsmanship Award in 1990.

In 1979 Redington and fellow Iditarod musher Susan Butcher took a team of seven huskies to the top of 20,320-foot Mount McKinley.

Redington mushed his last Iditarod in 1997, finishing in 36th place. The year marked the 50th year he had mushed on the trail and the 25th anniversary of the race.

Redington died June 24, 1999, at the age of 82. After his death, a new award was created in his honor, a bronze bust awarded for the first time to Doug Swingley in 2000. The Millennium Hotel, then known as the Regal Alaskan, one of the Iditarod sponsors, renamed its main ballroom after him. He was buried just as he lived—in a dog sled. And at Iditarod Trail Committee board meetings, his name is still listed for roll call; he is excused as "out on the trail."

Dorothy G. Page

Dorothy G. Page, "Mother of the Iditarod," and editor of the *Iditarod Runner* magazine for many years, died unexpectedly at her Wasilla, Alaska, home on Nov. 16, 1989. At the time of her death, she was treasurer of the Iditarod Trail Committee and was active in the Wasilla-Knik-Willow Creek Historical Society. She also served as curator of the Wasilla Museum.

An award in her honor is given annually at the Awards Banquet in Nome. The GCI Dorothy G. Page Award recognizes the musher who first reaches the halfway point in the race. The winner receives $3,000 and his or her name is engraved on a permanent trophy that is housed at the Iditarod headquarters in Wasilla. (Source: *Iditarod Silver* / Epicenter Press)

THE EARLY DAYS

When the first Saturday in March 1973 arrived, 34 dog teams lined up at the Anchorage starting line, at the then-called Tudor Track sprint complex. As they set out on the trail, the real issue was whether anyone at all would finish. A feeling of excitement pervaded the mushers, a feeling of being in on the ground floor of something

Red Olson and his team carried the Red Lantern as the 1974 last-place finisher. In good humor, he and fellow musher Joel Kottke carried signs as they crossed the finish line. Kottke's said "The"; Olson's said "End." Olson later carved the first burled arch that marked the end of the race.

new, perhaps a once-in-a-lifetime race. No one had raced huskies 1,000 or more miles.

At the first Iditarod pre-race banquet, George Attla of North Pole, the ten-time world sprint-mushing champion, announced he had conferred with Athabascan elders for an estimate of how long it should take the dogs to run to Nome. The race, proclaimed Attla, would take ten days. Attla and the elders were right—but it took most of two decades for the race to evolve into a ten-day event. The first ten-day Iditarod winning time was recorded in 1992, when Martin Buser of Big Lake notched his first victory. The mushers of 1973 truly headed off into the unknown.

Twenty days and 49 minutes later, Dick Wilmarth crossed the finish line in Nome, the winner of the debut Iditarod. Bobby Vent was 2nd, Dan Seavey, 3rd, and Attla, 4th.

One characteristic emerged in the first Iditarod and has persisted. The race was for everybody, the fast and the slow. For many, the most coveted prize of all was just earning a finisher's Iditarod belt buckle.

Of the 34 teams that started the 1973 race, 22 completed the run to Nome. John Schultz finished in 32 days, 5 hours, nearly two weeks behind Wilmarth. Schultz was the first recipient of a special prize that is still awarded—he won the initial Red Lantern, awarded to the final finisher of each year's race.

At the finishers' banquet in Nome that first year, Redington asked if they should do it again the next year. A mighty roar went up. The Iditarod was established. (Source: *Iditarod Silver* / Epicenter Press)

NATIONAL HISTORIC TRAIL STATUS

The 2,200 miles of winter trails associated with the Iditarod National Historic Trail are administered through the Anchorage Field Office of the federal Bureau of Land Management. A sign in Seward marks the beginning of the historic, 900-mile Seward-to-Nome segment that was used by Alaska Natives, prospectors, freight and mail carriers, and other winter travelers. It was mapped as early as 1908.

The late Sen. Ernest Gruening first proposed the Iditarod as a National Trail. But it wasn't until early 1977 that Sen. Mike Gravel introduced a bill designating the Iditarod Trail as the nation's first Historic Trail. In 1978, President Jimmy Carter signed the National Historic Trail Bill, which included the Iditarod Trail. Today the Iditarod is one of several National Historic Trails, among them the Oregon, Mormon, Pioneer, Lewis & Clark, Over Mountain, Victory, Nez Perce, Santa Fe, Trail of Tears, Juan Bautista and the Pony Express Trail.

For more information, browse the BLM website at www.blm.gov/ak/iditarod.

SECTION 2

Iditarod Through the Years

Joee Redington, Jr., son of the race cofounder, had already made a name for himself in the Alaska sprint circuit before entering the 1974 Iditarod and finishing in the Top 10.

Wien Collection, B85-27-1483, Anchorage Museum at Rasmuson Center

1973 Some 35 mushers set out from Anchorage in the inaugural race, unsure if any of them will reach Nome. But 22 people finish. Dick Wilmarth of Red Devil wins the inaugural in just over 20 days. He never races again. Last-place finisher John Schultz records the slowest Iditarod finish ever, more than 32 days. Among the competitors is sprint-dog racing legend George Attla, who ends up 4th. Race founder Joe Redington mortgages his Knik home to get the money for the purse.

1974 Carl Huntington wins in 20 days, 15 hours—becoming the only musher to ever win both the Iditarod and the Anchorage Fur Rendezvous World Championship sprint race. Joe Redington enters his first race and finishes 11th, losing a family battle to son

Joee Redington, Jr., who is 9th. Mary Shields and Lolly Medley become the first women to run. Some 41 percent of the starters (18) scratch.

1975 "Yukon Fox" Emmitt Peters of Ruby takes a huge chunk off the race record, winning in less than 14 days, 15 hours—about six days faster than the previous year. No musher will go faster until 1980. Despite Peters' time, his margin of victory is narrow— Jerry Riley of Nenana and Joee Redington are less than an hour behind. Joe Redington, Sr., records the first of his four 5th-place finishes—the highest he ever attained.

1976 Riley wins in almost 18 days, 23 hours to capture the lowest purse in Iditarod history—just $7,200. The man who nipped him the previous year, Emmitt Peters, finishes 5th. Years later, Riley will be banned for life amid accusations he struck a dog with a snow hook. Brash young rookie Rick Swenson of Manley finishes 10th.

1977 Rick Swenson, who will go on to become the Iditarod's winningest musher, takes the first of five victories in a very tight finish. He nips defending champ Riley by just five minutes, and finishes just 17 minutes ahead of Warner Vent.

1978 Dick Mackey of Wasilla noses out Swenson in a wild dash down Front Street in Nome. The one-second victory is the closest ever. There is finish line confusion about who won. Mackey gets the first lead dog across the finish line, but Swenson's sled crosses first. Judges rule that in a dog race the first dog wins. Rookie Susan Butcher finishes 19th—earning $600 of what will eventually become more than $377,000 in race winings. William "Sonny" Nelson of Ekwok and all of but two of his dogs are killed in an airplane crash on the way to the race. Nelson's dog handler, James Brandon, races in Nelson's honor.

1979 Swenson becomes the race's first two-time winner, edging Peters by just 42 minutes. The race marks a string of near misses for Peters. Following his championship, he finishes 5th, 4th, 3rd and 2nd in consecutive races. Butcher becomes the first woman to crack the Top 10 with a 9th-place finish.

Rick Swenson would one day set the record for the greatest number of Iditarod championships.

© 2006 Jeff Schultz / AlaskaStock.com

1980 Joe May, 5th a year earlier, vaults to the top with a 14-day, 7-hour run—the fastest since Peters' championship in 1975. Among the also rans are: Joe Garnie (12th), Larry "Cowboy" Smith (13th), Libby Riddles (18th), Martin Buser (22nd) and DeeDee Jonrowe (24th). Twenty-five mushers scratch, an Iditarod record.

1981 Swenson eats up the trail and pushes the race another step faster with his third victory in 12 days, 9 hours, as the prize money for first place doubles from $12,000 to $24,000. Swenson buddy Sonny Lindner and Roger Nordlum are less than an hour behind. Jeff King manages a 24th-place finish in his rookie run.

1982 Swenson continues his mastery of tight races, beating Susan Butcher to the line by less than four minutes. The top three mushers are just 12 minutes apart; the top 15 are just 11 hours apart. Herbie Nayokpuk, nicknamed "The Shishmaref Cannonball" in honor of his hometown, is beaten by a storm while trying to fight through a blizzard to victory. Other racers sit out the storm in Shaktoolik. Nayokpuk barely struggles back there alive after hours alone on the sea ice.

1983 Larry "Cowboy" Smith from Dawson, Yukon Territory, runs alone at the front of the race for hundreds of miles from the Alaska Range to the Bering Sea coast, but then is finally caught by Rick Mackey and Eep Anderson. Mackey eventually edges Anderson to become part of the only father-son duo of Iditarod champions (Dick Mackey won the 1978 race). Smith finishes third.

Libby Riddles
makes history
in 1985.
© 2006 Jeff Schultz /
AlaskaStock.com

Sprint-mushing champion Roxy Woods (later Roxy Wright Champaine) finishes a disappointing 23rd in her try at the longer race.

1984 Dean Osmar of Clam Gulch pioneers a front-running strategy to win the race in just over 12 days, 15 hours after Susan Butcher unexpectedly bolts out of the Rohn checkpoint. She has the mandatory 24-hour rest almost completed when she leaves to chase Swenson. Osmar says in Rohn that he thinks Butcher has just given him the race. He's right. Butcher finishes 2nd, Joe Garnie (3rd), Rick Swenson (6th), Joe Redington (7th). Defending champion Rick Mackey plummets to 29th.

1985 Libby Riddles, Garnie's mushing partner from Teller, becomes the first woman to win the Iditarod, charging alone into an arctic storm on Norton Sound. Her stunning victory brings new attention to the race. In a storm-plagued year, it takes Riddles more than 18 days to reach Nome, the slowest finishing time between 1977 and today. "Was Libby's win important?" asks longtime Iditarod Trail Committeeman Leo Rasmussen of Nome. "To tell you it wasn't would be telling you the greatest lie on earth." Butcher, long expected to be the first woman to win, watches the race from the sidelines after a moose stomps her team on the way to Skwentna.

1986 Butcher wins the first of four Iditarod victories after a tough battle with Garnie. He finishes 2nd, driving many of the same dogs that produced the championship the year before. With better weather along the trail, 45 of the 55 finishers get to Nome in better time than champion Riddles did the year before.

1987 Butcher knocks about 13 hours off her 1986 time to win again. Swenson pushes her all the way up the Bering Sea Coast, hoping the pressure will make her fold. She doesn't; he does. His dogs refuse to leave the Safety checkpoint. When they won't go, Swenson elects go to into the bar and have a drink. Butcher mushes alone under the burled arch in Nome. Swenson follows her in about four hours later. After several futile races with teams of Siberian huskies, future champion Martin Buser of Big Lake breaks into the Top 10 with a string of Rondy sprint dogs turned marathoners. He finishes in 12 days, 2 hours.

1988 In a dominating display, Butcher completes her trifecta, this time beating Swenson by more than half a day—with Buser 3rd and Garnie 4th. The four-consecutive victories by a woman leave fans wondering if a man will ever win again. Joe Redington finishes 5th for the fourth time in his career—a remarkable achievement at age 71.

1989 Butcher leads the race to the halfway point at Iditarod, but falls victim to what is thought to be a halfway jinx. Joe Runyan of Nenana, who'd dropped out the previous year, passes her and goes on to win by 68 minutes. Swenson is 3rd, continuing an unmatched string of Top-5 finishes.

1990 Butcher reclaims the top spot, her fourth victory in five years. No other Iditarod musher has ever had a decade of such dominance. "Libby's win started it," says fellow musher DeeDee Jonrowe. "Susan's reign cemented it. They showed it's possible for women to excel on an equal playing field. Libby's win captured the hearts of people who thought only an incredible mountain man could accomplish it."

1991 Swenson returns to become the incredible mountain man, battling his way through a White Mountain snowstorm so severe that Butcher, Runyan, and other veterans turn back. It is a record fifth Iditarod for Swenson. During the worst of it, he walks in front of his dog team, leading them through the storm. Why? "Desperation, I guess," he said. "I wanted to win the Iditarod." Martin Buser manages to fight his way through the same storm, only to finish a disappointing 2nd. Butcher waits for better weather and then leads in a group, including Runyan, who were earlier thought to have a lock on the top positions.

1992 Buser begins his string of three victories, breaking the 11-day barrier and leaving Butcher, Swenson and Tim Osmar in his wake. Future champion Jeff King breaks into the Top 10 for the first time with a 6th-place finish.

1993 King vaults to the championship in 10 days, 15 hours, the fastest to date. Jonrowe is just 32 minutes behind and former champion Rick Mackey takes 3rd. Swenson falls to 9th, his worst finish in a decade. Led by Buser and King, the top racers are beginning to experiment with a new breed of dogs, and a different style of competition, running faster between checkpoints and resting more between runs.

1994 Buser takes his second championship, beating Rick Mackey and defending-champion King. Butcher drops to 10th place and retires after the race. It is her lowest finish since her rookie season of 1978. Swenson climbs back into 4th.

1995 Doug Swingley of Montana makes history, becoming the first non-Alaskan to win the Iditarod in what remains the record time—less than 9 days, 3 hours. The Top-10 mushers all make it to Nome in under 10 days.

1996 King captures his second Iditarod, edging Swingley and Buser. A huge controversy erupts when a Swenson dog dies in harness for the first time in his 21 races. Swenson is withdrawn from the race, which leads to a battle with Iditarod officials that has Swenson threatening to never race again. Ultimately, Swenson wins, the rule is rewritten, and Swenson is scheduled to return for the 1998 race.

1997 Buser wins the 25th-anniversary Iditarod in less than 9 days, 9 hours to join Swenson and Butcher as the only mushers to win the race at least three times. Swingley is 2nd and King is 3rd. "A bunch of really talented athletes," Buser calls his 16-dog team, 10 of which finished. "If there was a humanoid who could do half as much as any of my dogs, they would be the world's greatest athletes at whatever they chose." Before the race, Buser, 38, had to let go of many of the animals that had carried him to his 1992 and 1994 victories. "He was pretty emotionally tied to that team," said

Charlie Boulding of Manley, Alaska.

June Price

his wife, Kathy Chapoton. "A few days before the race he told me this team was better than the 1992 team. That was an incredible thing for him to admit."

1998 Jeff King wins the 26th Iditarod in an official time of 9 days, 5 hours, 52 minutes. DeeDee Jonrowe and Charlie Boulding finish 2nd and 3rd respectively. With previous wins in 1993 and 1996, 1998 is King's third Iditarod victory. The 26th Iditarod Trail Sled Dog Race begins with balmy days. But for King, the final stretch ends in a gauntlet of roaring wind and whipping snow. It was the kind of storm, a battered and wind-burned King recalls later in Nome, that "I've only heard described by people. It was the longest couple hours of my life."

1999 Montana musher Doug Swingley claims his second Iditarod title by building a commanding lead at the race's halfway point and never looking back. At 45 years old, Swingley becomes the oldest musher to win the race and only the fifth competitor to win more than one Iditarod. Swingley completes the 27th running of the Iditarod in 9 days, 14 hours and 31 minutes. Three-time champion Martin Buser arrives in Nome in 2nd place more than 8 hours after Swingley. Buser completes the southern route of the 1,100-mile race in 9 days, 23 hours and 10 minutes.

2000 In back-to-back wins, Doug Swingley is first to the burled arch, proving once more that his innovative training methods pay off when it's time to turn up the heat. First to Ruby, then first to Nome in a record 9 days and 58 minutes. And speaking of heat, while the competitors prepared for the usual cold-weather surprises along the trail, some mushers didn't even use their mittens this year. According to former champion Joe Runyan, now reporting for Cabelas's online site, "The weather may have been for cream puffs, but the trail took a few sucker punches at the unsuspecting." Paul Gebhardt, Ramy Brooks, Jeff King, and Charlie Boulding arrive in Nome within hours of each other, rounding out the Top 5.

2001 Sixty-eight teams leave Fourth Avenue on March 3 and face the challenges of an icy trail with little to no snow in spots. Headwinds on the Yukon River as well as the coast also blast the mushers. Doug Swingley takes the lead early, reaching the halfway point first, and running what some are calling "the same race he did in 2000 and 1999," stretching his lead until he is unbeatable. "It's easy to predict what I'm going to do, but it's real hard to keep up," Swingley tells a CNN reporter. If not for poor trail conditions, Swingley might have broken his record time from 2000. He finishes in 9 days, 19 hours, 55 minutes and 50 seconds. Willow musher Linwood Fiedler slides into Nome in 2nd place at 10 days, 3 hours, 58 minutes and 57 seconds. Former champions Jeff King and Rick Swenson finish in 3rd and 4th, respectively.

2002 In his 19th running of the Iditarod, Martin Buser rebounds from a disappointing 24th place in 2001 to run the fastest race in Iditarod history, busting through the 9-day barrier and finishing with happy, healthy dogs in 8 days, 22 hours, 46 minutes and 2 seconds. Observers at the checkpoints characterize him as a "machine," with no wasted effort as he feeds, beds, and massages and booties his dogs. Mere hours separate the mushers who follow Buser into Nome: Ramy Brooks arriving in 9 days, 9 hours, 49

2004 Champion
Mitch Seavey and
wife Janine wait in
the starting chute of
the 2005 race.
June Price

minutes, 18 seconds, with John Baker just five hours later, and Jon
Little two hours behind Baker.

2003 The race restart moves to Fairbanks this year due to
unusually warm weather conditions in Southcentral. From
Fairbanks, the mushers follow a trail to the Yukon River and
onward to Ruby, where they pick up what is normally the Northern
Route. At Kaltag, they make a loop to Anvik and back to Kaltag,
then take the regular trail to Nome. Robert Sørlie of Norway and
Ramy Brooks are in a two-man race out of White Mountain, but
Sørlie reigns, arriving in Nome in 9 days, 15 hours, 47 minutes
and 36 seconds, making him the Iditarod's first international
champion. Contender Brooks claims 2nd place for the second year
in a row, finishing in 9 days, 17 hours, 37 minutes and 10 seconds.

2004 Representing the second generation in an Alaskan
mushing family, Mitch Seavey triumphs in the 32nd Iditarod with
a time of 9 days, 12 hours, 22 minutes and 22 seconds. Seavey
grew up in Seward, at Mile 0 of the Iditarod Trail. His father, Dan,
ran the first race in 1973 and continues to serve on the ITC board.
The third generation includes Danny and Tyrell, who have each
completed the Iditarod, and Dallas, who placed 4th in this year's
Junior Iditarod. Three-time Iditarod champion Jeff King, who

The Redington legacy
continued in 2005 as Ray
Redington, Jr., grandson of
race cofounder Joe
Redington, Sr., prepared to
run his fifth race. At left is
his father, Raymie
Redington, who entered the
first Iditarod and has
finished 11 races.
June Price

arrived two hours behind Seavey, this year introduced his newest
innovation in sled design, adding a compartment that doubles as a
seat and storage. Dubbed the Old Man Sled, or the Tail Dragger, the
sled remains lightweight, yet relieves the musher from standing the
whole time. Rounding out the Top 5 are Norwegian Kjetil Backen in
3rd, Ramey Smyth in 4th, and Ed Iten in 5th.

2005 Breaking trail in warm weather was the brutal task of
frontrunner Robert Sørlie this year as soft, sugary snow covered
hundreds of miles before him. Still, Sørlie and his 8-dog team looked
strong when they arrived in Nome, completing the race in 9 days,
18 hours, 39 minutes and 13 seconds, and honoring his native
Norway with a second championship. Just 34 minutes later, Ed Iten
claimed 2nd place, his best finish yet, and breathing down his neck
was Mitch Seavey, with only 7 minutes separating them. Jon Little,
reporting for Cabela's online, summarized the top three mushers
this way: "Sørlie is a consummate musher, relying on his unflagging
positive outlook and ability to go without sleep for days on end to
pilot a winning team. His mantra is 'no problem' and he combines
that outlook with warm charm, a rich sense of humor and loads of
physical toughness. In fact, those traits are common among the top
three dog teams this year. Iten and Seavey also are gentlemen. They

combine character, gentleness, humor and wit. Like many teams at the front of the pack, they are also true racers."

2006 Doug Swingley, ever characterized by the media as "cocky Swingley," claims the halfway award once more. Jeff King picks up the gauntlet, however, and running down the Yukon, it looks as if the race could go to either of the two veteran champions. However in blizzard conditions near Unalakleet, King's dogs still have their pep, while Swingley's are tiring. While King charges ahead, Swingley decides a rest is in order, and King takes his fourth victory after 9 days, 11 hours, 11 minutes, 36 seconds on the trail. In post-race interviews, King gives credit to his leader, Salem, for stopping the team when it briefly got away from him near Kaltag. The incident could have cost him the race, he says. Swingley and crew arrive in 2nd at 9 days, 14 hours, 18 minutes, and 20 seconds. Paul Gebhardt, DeeDee Jonrowe and John Baker complete the Top 5 roster. The 50-year-old King is also crowned with yet another title: oldest champion in Iditarod history.

(Sources 1973-1999: *Anchorage Daily News* / Mike Campbell; 2000-2006: iditarod.com; cabelas.com; cnn.com)

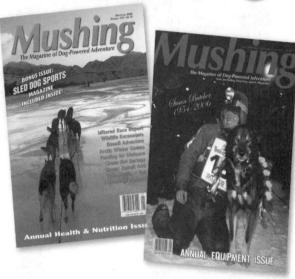

The Race Today

AWARDS

Each year a number of special awards are given to mushers in the Iditarod. For the 2006 race, the following awards were given:

Lolly Medley Golden Harness Award: Hand-made embroidered harness recognizing the outstanding lead dog of the race. Presentation honors harness-maker Lolly Medley, one of two women to run the second Iditarod in 1974. Medley personally awarded the Golden Harness every year until her death in 1997. It is now presented in her memory by the city of Nome.

Alaska Airlines Leonhard Seppala Humanitarian Award: To the musher who has best demonstrated outstanding care of his or her team through the race while remaining competitive. Selected by veterinary staff and race officials. Lead crystal cup on an illuminated wooden base and two free round-trip tickets to anywhere Alaska Airlines flies.

Rookie of the Year: A $1,500 cash prize and trophy to the top-placing man or woman racing his or her first Iditarod.

Fred Meyer Sportsmanship Award: Each musher selected receives a $1,000 gift certificate and an engraved glass trophy.

Global Information Technologies Most Improved Musher Award: Recognizes the most improved musher with a trophy and the use of a satellite phone for a year.

Names of first- and last-place finishers are added to two perpetual trophies: the champions' trophy and the infamous Red Lantern Trophy. Yellow roses are draped over the shoulders of the champion's lead dogs at the finish line.

© 2006 Jeff Schultz / AlaskaStock.com

Chevron Most Inspirational Musher Award: Official finishers decide who among themselves was most inspirational on the trail. Winner receives a plaque and $1,000 in Chevron/Texaco gas.

PenAir Spirit of Alaska Award: A "spirit mask" and $500 credit toward airfare or freight shipments awarded to first musher to arrive in McGrath.

GCI Dorothy G. Page Halfway Award: Presented at Cripple, the halfway checkpoint in odd years when the race covers the southern route. Winner receives $3,000 in gold. A perpetual trophy made of Alaskan birch and marble, and featuring a photograph of the late Dorothy G. Page, remains year-round at Iditarod headquarters in Wasilla.

Wells Fargo Gold Coast Award: A trophy and $2,500 in gold nuggets goes to the first musher to arrive in Unalakleet, on the coast. A perpetual trophy commemorating the award remains year-round at the Iditarod headquarters in Wasilla.

Golden Clipboard Award: Awarded by the Iditarod Official Finishers Club to the best checkpoint on the trail.

Millennium Hotel's First Musher to the Yukon Award: A seven-course gourmet meal prepared by the Executive Chef of the

Millennium Hotel awaits the first musher to the Yukon River. The winner also receives $3,500 in cash.

Fastest Time from Safety to Nome: A long-standing award presented by the Nome Kennel Club, $500 goes to the musher who finishes in the top twenty and has the fastest time from Safety to Nome.

Anchorage Chrysler Dodge Official Truck Award: Keys to a fully loaded Dodge Ram 4x4 diesel truck are handed to the winner of the Iditarod Trail Sled Dog Race at the finish line in Nome.

Cabela's Outfitter Award: A $1,000 gift certificate and a Stihl chainsaw is awarded to each of two mushers who are selected in a random drawing.

Golden Stethoscope Award: Plaque presented by the Iditarod Official Finishers Club to a veterinarian on the trail.

Wells Fargo Red Lantern Award: The last musher across the finish line is presented with a Red Lantern and earns a place in Iditarod history.

BIB NO. 1

(See also: Honorary Mushers)

The Iditarod's connection to the historic Nenana-to-Nome Serum Run of 1925 was retained through the memory of Leonhard Seppala, the most famous of the diphtheria mushers. From the inaugural Iditarod in 1973 until 1980, bib No. 1 was assigned to Seppala to honor his role in that race against death. Every year since 1980, the Iditarod Trail Committeee has selected one or two people who have made a significant contribution to the sport (even if that person is not a musher). In the early 1980s, bib No. 1 went to other serum runners who were still living. Among them were Edgar Nollner, Edgar Kalland, Charlie Evans and Billy McCarty. Nollner was the last of the serum mushers to die. He passed away on Jan. 18, 1999.

In 1997, the Iditarod saw its 25th anniversary and race founder Joe Redington, Sr., celebrated the event, and his 80th birthday, by running the race again. Race organizers did not require him to participate in the starting-place drawing. Redington was given bib No. 1—the only competing musher in Iditarod history to have that honor—and the race was dedicated to him that year.

CHAMPIONS
(See: First-Place Winners, 1973-2006)

CHECKPOINTS
(See also: Section 3, The Checkpoints)
Mushers are required to stop at about two dozen places along the race route, some in villages, some at mere tents at a remote site. At certain checkpoints, a musher may choose to take the required 8-hour or 24-hour layover. At each stop, a checker/timer meets each musher for an official recording of the arrival time. Volunteer veterinarians examine the dogs, and volunteers assist in directing the musher to a place where the team can rest, and to the location of hot water and their food-drop bags, as well as a meal for the musher. Communications volunteers make reports from these remote sites throughout the race, media personnel grab interviews and photographs, and if a dog is unfit to continue, the Iditarod Air Force is directed to fly out dropped dogs. On his or her way out of the checkpoint, the musher must have the checker/timer present to make the departure time official.

COMMUNICATIONS
A major Iditarod sponsor in 2006, GIT Satellite Communications donated a full complement of Iridium Satellite equipment and airtime, including handheld satellite telephones and pagers for remote and mobile applications. According to a company representative, "The satellite phones can be used any place on the trail to contact air, headquarter or checkpoints. The pagers feature a broadcast capability allowing a message to be sent to all of the pagers at one time to provide updates or alerts to both ground and air volunteers. The docking stations allow for the safety and

Perennial volunteers at Rohn, "Sheriff Terry" and "Mayor Jasper" set up the satellite phone for checkpoint communications. Their reference manual, of course, is a copy of Red Green's book with directions on creative use of duct tape.
Jasper Bond

convenience of indoor installation at the checkpoints where field staff and volunteers are located around the clock. Both the satellite phones and the docking stations work with the data kits to support Internet and email capability. This allows personnel to download real-time weather reports, plot and communicate the location of the mushers, as well as communicate race status to news agencies around the world with both feature text and photographs."

The 2006 communications coordinator was Mark Kelliher (KL7TQ), who was charged with directing comms personnel all along the trail. In preparation for the race, volunteers were asked to study the Iditarod Trail Communications Handbook, which can be viewed online at http://home.gci.net/~kelliher/. The handbook offers details about how to pack, where volunteers can expect to sleep, how to format internet messages, and most importantly, what equipment works best and where/how to set up and transmit. To non-techies in the population, part of some entries may read like another language. For example, the Yentna Station checkpoint entry says: "This is the most hectic checkpoint on the trail. It is non-stop traffic from the first dog to the last. I recommend you sleep until you know the dogs are close. 1 ham around the corner to catch the out times and 1 at the arrival area to catch them when they arrive.

A crossband repeater (5/5w) on a small 3 el. beam at the lodge will access both repeaters 27/30 full quieting (25' coax). Handheld is marginal from the checkpoint. Hot stick mast required to hold antenna. Cell phone will not work."

DISTANCE

(See also: Section 3, The Checkpoints)

The race alternates on a northern and southern course each year. While each route exceeds 1,100 miles, the true distance changes annually, because the trail weaves in and out of the natural terrain and routing is often affected by the weather. Race officials use 1,049 as the symbolic distance: 1,000 miles, plus 49 to recognize Alaska as the 49th state to enter the union.

A bronze statue of Joe Redington, Sr., stands outside the ITC headquarters.

Ray Redington, Jr.

ENTRY FEE

The entry fee for the 2007 race was $1,850, and included Iditarod and Mush with P.R.I.D.E. membership dues. Mushers could sign up and pay the fee on or after June 24, 2006. The fee had to be received or postmarked by midnight, December 1, 2006. After that date, a musher could still pay the ITC a non-refundable fee to sign up, but had to wait for another musher to withdraw. No musher could sign up after February 16, 2007.

FATHER OF THE IDITAROD

(See also: Section 1, Movers and Shakers)

This honorary title was given to Joe Redington, Sr., who was instrumental in co-founding the race with Dorothy G. Page.

A bronze memorial statue of Redington was erected outside Iditarod headquarters, near Wasilla, Alaska, after Redington's death in 1999. Alaskan sculptor Joan Bugbee Jackson of Cordova worked from a Bill Devine photograph of Redington posing with one of his favorite sled dogs, Feets.

FINANCES

Sled-dog racing is an expensive sport. In the words of Dori Hollingsworth, a sprint musher from Seward, "Sprint racing is extremely addictive. Worse than cocaine and just as expensive." Minimum expenses for a musher to enter a team in the Iditarod is estimated at $15,000, but this figure can reach over $50,000 for a truly competitive team. Each dog in the kennel is worth $2,000 or more, and this figure increases to over $8,000 for a fully trained lead dog. Race expenses, including dog food, entry fees, harnesses, booties, and airfare for a long-distance race can easily exceed $10,000. Sleds, clothing and equipment that can be reused annually also are very spendy. Cabela's columnist and Iditarod musher Jon Little estimated $1,000 just for dog booties alone for the big race. Mushers living in rural areas pay significantly more for the upkeep of their kennels, as everything must be flown in, including themselves and their dogs for the beginning of the race. Although the Iditarod was founded to honor the many people who helped with the serum run, and the majority of those were Native Alaskans, fewer and fewer Natives and other rural residents have been able to enter the race due to the expense.

FOOD DROP

A vast army of volunteers on the ground, along with critical air support, aids in organizing and distributing advance shipments of food and supplies for mushers and their dogs. Before the race, each musher receives a supply of heavy-duty bags with checkpoint names stamped on them. They fill the bags with mandatory quantities of food and approved gear—more than 1,500 pounds of it—write their names on the sides, and deliver them to a distribution center in Anchorage. From there, the supplies are shipped out to most

FIRST-PLACE WINNERS, 1973-2006

YEAR	MUSHER	HOMETOWN	D/H/M/S
1973	Dick Wilmarth	Red Devil, AK	20:00:49:41
1974	Carl Huntington	Galena, AK	20:15:02:07
1975	Emmitt Peters	Ruby, AK	14:14:43:45
1976	Gerald Riley	Nenana, AK	18:22:58:17
1977	Rick Swenson	Manley, AK	16:16:27:13
1978	Dick Mackey	Wasilla, AK	14:18:52:24
1979	Rick Swenson	Manley, AK	15:10:37:47
1980	Joe May	Trapper Creek, AK	14:07:11:51
1981	Rick Swenson	Manley, AK	12:08:45:02
1982	Rick Swenson	Manley, AK	16:04:40:10
1983	Rick Mackey	Wasilla, AK	12:14:10:44
1984	Dean Osmar	Clam Gulch, AK	12:15:07:33
1985	Libby Riddles	Teller, AK	18:00:20:17
1986	Susan Butcher	Manley, AK	11:15:06:00
1987	Susan Butcher	Manley, AK	11:02:05:13
1988	Susan Butcher	Manley, AK	11:11:41:40
1989	Joe Runyan	Nenana, AK	11:05:24:34
1990	Susan Butcher	Manley, AK	11:01:53:23
1991	Rick Swenson	Two Rivers, AK	12:16:34:39
1992	Martin Buser	Big Lake, AK	10:19:17:00
1993	Jeff King	Denali, AK	10:15:38:15
1994	Martin Buser	Big Lake, AK	10:13:02:39
1995	Doug Swingley	Simms, MT	09:02:42:19
1996	Jeff King	Denali, AK	09:05:43:13
1997	Martin Buser	Big Lake, AK	09:08:30:45
1998	Jeff King	Denali, AK	09:05:52:26
1999	Doug Swingley	Lincoln, MT	09:14:31:07
2000	Doug Swingley	Lincoln, MT	09:00:58:06
2001	Doug Swingley	Lincoln, MT	09:19:55:50
2002	Martin Buser	Big Lake, AK	08:22:46:02
2003	Robert Sørlie	Norway	09:15:47:36
2004	Mitch Seavey	Seward, AK	09:12:20:22
2005	Robert Sørlie	Norway	09:18:39:31
2006	Jeff King	Denali, AK	09:11:11:36

FIRST-PLACE CASH PRIZE, 1973-2006			
YEAR	AMOUNT	YEAR	AMOUNT
1973	$12,000	1990	$50,000
1974	$12,000	1991	$50,000
1975	$15,000	1992	$51,600
1976	$ 7,200	1993	$50,000
1977	$ 9,600	1994	$50,000
1978	$12,000	1995	$52,500
1979	$12,000	1996	$50,000
1980	$12,000	1997	$50,000
1981	$24,000	1998	$51,000
1982	$24,000	1999	$60,000
1983	$24,000	2000	$60,000
1984	$24,000	2001	$62,857
1985	$50,000	2002	$62,857
1986	$50,000	2003	$68,571
1987	$50,000	2004	$69,000
1988	$30,000	2005	$72,067
1989	$50,000	2006	$69,000

checkpoints along the route. During the race, checkpoint volunteers direct the mushers to their stash of bags.

FOOD, Mushers

Ultimately, a driver's choice of food for himself is his own decision. Items such as frozen pizza, cheeseburgers and hot dogs seem to be popular. Salami makes a good choice because it is high in fat, contains much protein, and stores well. Honey, chocolate and high-carbohydrate foods are useful for the energy they produce. The most popular beverages on the trail are water and coffee, although Gatorade and other electrolyte-replenishing sports drinks and the occasional caffeinated soda are popular as well.

Food-drop
bags ready for
shipping out
to Skwentna
and Elim.
June Price

According to author Mary Hood, mushers should carry as much as 19 percent body fat, as they have been known to lose as many as 25 to 30 pounds during the race. Most need to consume between 8,000 and 10,000 calories per day to compensate for heat loss and heavy exertion. Pressures of the race and the trail can result in mushers neglecting their own diets, according to Hood—hence the dramatic weight loss.

HAZARDS

Mushing 1,100 miles across Alaska's wilderness is not without hazards. Mushers may encounter wild animals, including moose, bison, caribou and wolves. Tree branches may block the trail. Overflow or thin ice may hide frigid water on the trail. Heavy snows, whiteout conditions and even blizzards may make seeing the trail nearly impossible. Dogs can run away, attempt mating, or lose the trail. Very cold weather means frostbite and hypothermia are possible. Hard-driving mushers risk falling asleep or falling off the sled.

Overflow. Cracks and thinning ice sometimes allow water to flow onto the surface of a frozen body of water. Even the most experienced winter traveler may be caught off guard—unsure if the ice is open, or if the water is merely a thin layer on top of safe ice. Every musher has stories about breaking through or at least getting wet due to overflow.

Weather. Weather is hard to predict along the Iditarod Trail in March. Possible temperature extremes range from 45° F to -60° F.

Snowfall can vary too, depending on the winter and the region. An average of 80 inches of snow falls annually in the McGrath area, but the Farewell Burn can have patches of open ground. Winds along the Norton Sound can cause a windchill factor of -100° F, and blizzards have halted many mushers several years.

To keep themselves and their dogs safe, mushers must pay close attention to weather conditions, and most are aware of the following "rules":

30-30-30 rule. At -30° F with winds of 30 mph, human flesh freezes solid in 30 seconds.

50-50-50 rule. In water temperatures of 50°, a person has 50 percent chance of surviving for 50 minutes.

Whiteout. When the wind is whipping during a fine snowfall, resulting blizzard conditions blend the ground and the sky into a world of crystallized white. On the ground or in the air, any traveler can suffer a dangerous case of disorientation, getting lost, following the wrong trail, and losing all sense of direction.

Wild Animals. In the course of mushing more than a thousand miles across the Last Frontier, you'd think the teams would see more animals than they do. On the other hand, the Iditarod infrastructure—from set-up to the race to takedown—generates a human presence and activity level that wild animals instinctively avoid. Still, big game in particular poses a hazard.

Bison. An often-snowless area just north of Rohn is known as the Buffalo Tunnels, a stretch that's infamous for rocky terrain and possible encounters with a herd of wild bison. According to the Bureau of Land Management, the Farewell bison herd, as it's called, numbers about 300 animals. In an interview with Scholastic.com, Martin Buser recalled the time his team ran after a small herd of bison in the Farewell Burn and took him on a wild ride. Since there was no snow that year, Buser said, most of what he saw were clouds of dust as the animals ran away.

Moose. Moose may be encountered anywhere along the Iditarod Trail. Alaska's largest mammal, bulls may weigh between 1,200 and

Wolf tracks intersect the Iditarod Trail near Ophir.
BLM / Kevin Keeler

1,600 pounds; cows are 800 to 1,300 pounds. Only bulls carry antlers, which are shed each fall and then regrown. Although moose are not generally aggressive, they are unpredictable, and cows with calves are fiercely protective. In areas with deep snow, they may seek out hard-packed trails for easier going, then show reluctance to give way to oncoming dog teams.

Inevitably, Iditarod mushers have had encounters with moose. In 1985, a moose attacked Susan Butcher's team, killing two of her dogs and injuring thirteen, forcing her to scratch from the race. Many fans believe Butcher might have won the race that year if not for the attack.

In 1980, Jerry Austin and Dick Mackey had to kill a moose that attacked their teams. They were charged with wasting the meat, but the charges were dropped. And in 1995, Austin stopped a charging moose with an explosive shot fired from a flare pistol.

Caribou. Top Iditarod competitor Paul Gebhardt had has his share of unpleasant wildlife sightings, from spotting a polar bear on his rookie run, to losing a lead dog to an enraged moose, to to running through more than one herd of caribou.

The Western Caribou Herd is one of the largest in the state, and one part of the herd, as many as 50,000 animals, may be found in the eastern part of the Seward Peninsula during the winter months.

Wolves. These shy creatures will avoid people and dog teams if possible, but mushers occasionally see signs of them. Martin Buser remembered seeing one wolf in what he called a "rare instance."

Another time, he saw evidence of a wolf pack in the area, but didn't see the animals themselves.

HONORARY MUSHERS
(See: Section 7, Unforgettable People)

IDITA-RIDER PROGRAM
Fans can bid for the privilege of riding in a musher's sled during the first stretch of the race from Anchorage to Eagle River, about 11 miles. The ITC fund-raiser generates prize money of up to $1,049

Musher G.B. Jones, Waldo, and 2004 Idita-Rider Betty Walden.
June Price

for each musher finishing below 30th place. The benefit auction begins in November of each year, and interested riders can bid online at www.iditarod.com. Minimum bids are $500; you can secure a ride with your favorite musher for a flat $7,500. In its first twelve years, the program raised more than $1.1 million.

IDITAROD AIR FORCE
Volunteer pilots fly through some of the nation's worst weather to transport food, supplies, people and dogs along the trail. They have become known as the Iditarod Air Force. These pilots use their own planes and the Iditarod Trail Committee pays for gas, oil and insurance (often with donations from specific sponsors). They receive assistance on bigger loads from commercial airlines as well.

Usually experienced Alaskan pilots, members of the Iditarod Air Force have a remarkable safety record. For the 2006 race, chief pilot John Norris said, "Our volunteer pilots collectively bring 731 years and 251,931 hours of flying experience to the table." The Iditarod Air Force crew for the 2006 race included:

Chief Pilot John Norris, Cessna 180
Martin Carlson, Cessna 185
Bob Elliot, 1969 Cessna 180
Wes Erb, Cessna 170B
Danny Davidson, Cessna 180
Richard Dowling, Cessna 185
Russ Dunlap, Cessna 180
Robert "Bear" Hanson, Piper 20/22
Glenn Hanson, Cessna 182
Steve Hakala, Cessna 185
Ken Kastner, Cessna 180
Jim Kintz, Cessna 180
Ed Kornfield, Cessna 180
Mike Koskovich, Cessna 185

Jon Van Zyle, Iditarod's
official artist, designed the
Iditarod Air Force logo.

Monte Mabry, Cessna 185
Bill Mayer, Cessna 185
Phil Morgan, Cessna 185
Bruce Moroney, Cessna 185
Diana Moroney, Cessna 185
Rich Mullowney, Cessna 185
George Murphy, Aeronica
Greg Niesen, Cessna 180
Dale Olsen, 1970 Cessna 180H
Joe Pendergrass, Cessna 180
Mike Petrie, Cessna 180
Frank Pinkerton, Cessna 172
Joe Pientka, Cessna Caravan (PenAir)
Gary Quarles, Cessna 180
Reagan Russey, 1966 Cessna 180H
Tim Skala, Cessna 185
Chris Urstadt, Cessna 185

The pilots work closely with volunteer "load coordinators,"
assisted in 2006 by communications coordinator Mark Kelliher

(KL7TQ). Other load coordinator volunteers included Wendy Strom, Petie Peterson, Hannelore Kelliher (NL7EA) and Lin Perry-Plake Hjortstorp (WL7JI).

IDITAROD HALL OF FAME

In 1997, The *Anchorage Daily News* established the Iditarod Hall of Fame to mark the 25th anniversary of the race.

Nominations come from readers and from a committee established by the *Daily News*. Each committee member has extensive knowledge of the race. Journalists who have covered the race for many years make the final selections. Since 1997, the following individuals have been named to the Hall of Fame:

Jerry Austin
Don Bowers
Martin Buser
Susan Butcher
Joe Delia
DeeDee Jonrowe
Dick Mackey
Herbie Nayokpuk
Emmitt Peters
Leo Rasmussen
Joe Redington, Sr.
Libby Riddles
Bob Sept
Rick Swenson
Doug Swingley
Jon Van Zyle

IDITAROD TRAIL COMMITTEE

The Iditarod Trail Committee is a 501 (c) 3 non-profit corporation, overseen by a Board of Directors, which relies on volunteers and donations to launch a major event each year. The 2005-06 board included:

President: Richard Burmeister
Vice President: Lee Larsen
Secretary: Jim Palin
Treasurer: Rick Swenson
Directors:
    Sam Maxwell
    John Handeland
    Mark Moderow
    Dan Seavey
    Mike Owens

The permanent staff, based in Wasilla, is comprised of a handful of people who are aided by hundreds of volunteers. The staff for 2006 included:

Stan Hooley is the Executive Director of the Iditarod.
June Price

Executive Director: Stan Hooley
Assistant to the Executive Director:
    Starre Szelag
Director of Public Relations:
    Chas St. George
Development Director: Greg Bill
Race Director: Joanne Potts
Chief Veterinarian:
    Stuart Nelson, Jr., D.V.M.
Race Marshal: Mark Nordman
Membership, Iditarider, and Restart:
    Deby Trosper
Volunteer Coordinator: Lois Harder

The budget for the 2006 race was $3.7 million, which covered the purse, operating expenses and overhead, and shipping food and supplies (as much as 150,000 pounds total) to checkpoints.

The race marshal is the top race official, and is usually someone with extensive experience in dog mushing and racing. He is assisted by a staff of race judges.

In all, as many as 1,800 volunteers participate in the race each year, many of whom leave their jobs and devote their hard-earned vacation days for the pleasure of working behind the scenes.

Checkpoint volunteers include checker/timers, veterinarians, and communications specialists, among others. Volunteer trailbreakers ride snowmachines about six hours ahead of the mushers, breaking the trail and, where necessary, marking it with four-foot pieces of wooden lath with colored reflecting tape. The Iditarod Trail Committee pays their expenses.

In both Anchorage or Nome, volunteers arrange pre- or post-race banquets and social events, handle the publicity, care for dropped dogs, handle the telephones, operate concession stands, solicit donations, work with sponsors, coordinate with city, state and federal agencies, and perform dozens of other tasks—small and large—required to put on such a major event.

IDITAROD HEADQUARTERS

The Iditarod Trail Sled Dog Race headquarters, or simply HQ, as many call it, is located at Mile 2.2 Knik Road outside of Wasilla, Alaska. The impressive log-cabin structure, built in 1986, includes corporate offices as well as a small museum dedicated to the race. There's a gift shop, videos, portraits of famous mushers, and the infamous "Red Lantern Award" inscribed with the names of past winners. In addition, the mounts of two famous dogs are permanently installed here: Togo, the Leonhard Seppala dog that led him through many rough miles during the 1925 serum run; and Andy, the renowned leader of five-time champion Rick Swenson.

Summertime visitors to the headquarters may visit a replica of the Rohn checkpoint on the grounds and take a ride behind a team of sled dogs pulling a wheeled cart. A statue of Joe Redington, Sr., near the entrance of the headquarters honors the "Father of the Iditarod," and his dedication to mushing dogs.

JUNIOR IDITAROD

Dallas Seavey ran in the 2005 Junior Iditarod, then turned 18 one day before the Iditarod, qualifying him to enter both races in the same year. He is the youngest musher in race history.
June Price

The Junior Iditarod is an annual event that's launched one weekend prior to the "big race," the Iditarod, and mushers from 14 to 17 years old make a round trip along a portion of the Iditarod Trail.

The Junior Iditarod was first run in March 1978, inspired by several young mushers: Karl Clauson, Kenny Pugh, Clarence Shockley, Rome Gilman, Mark Couch, Susan Wagnon, Clint Mayeur, Jessee Reynolds, and Eric Beeman.

In today's race, the mushers, many racing with their own teams, follow the Iditarod Trail for about 160 miles, starting in Wasilla, to the Big Bend area of the Yentna River. The Yentna Station Roadhouse is the halfway point. The junior drivers stay with their dogs during the overnight stop, caring for them just as the adult mushers do during the Iditarod.

The top three mushers, plus two other award-winners in sportsmanship and humanitarianism, share the purse of $10,000 in scholarship funds sponsored through the University of Alaska College Savings Plan. Many Junior Iditarod mushers have gone on to compete in the Iditarod, including Tim Osmar, three-time winner of the Junior Iditarod; Andy Willis, a three-time junior finisher; Kimarie Hansen, also a three-time junior finisher; as well as Karl Clauson, Rome Gilman, Clarence Shockley, Jason and Laird Barron, Aaron Burmeister, Simon Kineen, and Cim and Ramey Smyth.

Robert Sørlie does a sound check during a 2005 interview with the Outdoor Life Network.
June Price

Dallas Seavey is the only person to have competed in both the Junior Iditarod and the Iditarod in the same year, since his 18th birthday occurred between the two races in 2005.

MEDIA COVERAGE

Sports reporters primarily covered the Iditarod from its first run in 1973 until 1985, when Libby Riddles became the first woman to win the race. Riddles' win—mushing to Nome in the teeth of a blizzard that halted the rest of the field—captured the attention of the nation.

Since then, the Iditarod has been covered by nearly every major news organization around the world, as well as by dozens of Alaskan reporters and photographers representing nearly every newspaper, television station and radio station across the state.

Covering the Iditarod is no small undertaking for any news organization. The Iditarod Air Force is often pressed into ferrying reporters and photographers from checkpoint to checkpoint. News organizations with bigger budgets charter their own aircraft so they can be sure their crews can move along the trail on their own schedule. For many years, film, videotapes and stories were flown back to Anchorage and the larger towns along the trail. The advent of email and websites, along with digital cameras and camcorders, means most information and images are transported electronically.

Nevertheless, reporters and photographers still face many of the same logistical and safety challenges as do the mushers along

Each year, the Iditarod's official artist, Jon Van Zyle, produces a limited edition of Iditarod posters.
Jon Van Zyle

the trail. But instead of keeping dogs safe and warm, they must baby their cameras and computers as they interview and photograph the mushers and their dogs.

OFFICIAL ARTIST
Jon Van Zyle

Jon Van Zyle is an internationally recognized wildlife artist who is closely identified with sled-dog racing in his home state of Alaska. Twice Van Zyle has run the Iditarod Trail Sled Dog Race from which he derived artistic inspiration for a magnificent series of original paintings, prints, and posters that capture the excitement and spirit of the annual race. More than 200 of his works have been published as limited edition prints and posters. He also has illustrated several children's books. Van Zyle and his wife, Jona, live in a cedar home near Eagle River, Alaska, and own a team of Siberian huskies. More of his work can be viewed at www.jonvanzyle.com. (Source: *Jon Van Zyle's Alaska Sketchbook* / Epicenter Press)

OFFICIAL PHOTOGRAPHER
Jeff Schultz

Jeff Schultz has been the official photographer of the Iditarod Trail Sled Dog Race since 1982, donating his time, energy, and talent to the event each year. An Alaskan since 1978, Schultz grew up in the San Francisco area, where he nurtured a love of the outdoors and photography. As a boy, he dreamed of building a log cabin and living off the land. At 18, he followed his dream north and launched his career as an outdoor photographer. Since then, Schultz's images have appeared worldwide in advertisements, books, corporate publications, and magazines, among them

National Geographic, Outside and *Sports Illustrated.* Schultz owns and operates Alaska Stock Images, representing more than 150 commercial photographers. He and his wife, Joan, and their two children, Ben and Hannah, make their home in Anchorage. (Source: *Iditarod Silver* / Epicenter Press)

P.R.I.D.E.

This acronym stands for "Proving Responsible Information on a Dog's Environment." The Mush with P.R.I.D.E. non-profit organization is based in Fairbanks, but its outreach extends all over the world, as each musher's entry fee in the Iditarod includes membership dues for P.R.I.D.E. and the Iditarod.

According to the Mush with P.R.I.D.E. website, the organization "supports the responsible care and humane treatment of all dogs and is dedicated to enhancing the care and treatment of sled dogs in their traditional and modern uses."

The group promotes educational efforts on sled-dog care, improved husbandry, veterinary practices. For more, browse their website at http://www.mushwithpride.org/.

PURSE

For the 2006 race, the purse, or total prize money paid to winners, was nearly $840,000. Of that, $794,800 went to teams finishing in 1st

1st Place	$69,000	11th Place	$32,300
2nd Place	$64,300	12th Place	$29,700
3rd Place	$59,800	13th Place	$27,300
4th Place	$55,600	14th Place	$25,000
5th Place	$51,700	15th Place	$22,800
6th Place	$48,000	16th Place	$20,700
7th Place	$44,400	17th Place	$18,800
8th Place	$41,100	18th Place	$17,000
9th Place	$38,000	19th Place	$15,300
10th Place	$35,100	20th Place	$13,600

21st Place	$12,100	26th Place	$ 5,700
22nd Place	$10,700	27th Place	$ 4,600
23rd Place	$ 9,300	28th Place	$ 3,600
24th Place	$ 8,000	29th Place	$ 2,700
25th Place	$ 6,800	30th Place	$ 1,800

through 30th place. All other finishers from 31st and onward received $1,049 in prize money.

RECORDS and FIRSTS

1974 Slowest winning time: Carl Huntington in 20 days, 15 hours, 2 minutes, 7 seconds.

1974 First woman to finish the race: Mary Shields

1978 First woman to place in the money: Susan Butcher, 19th place

1983 Largest field of rookies. By 2006, the record still held.

1983 Two generations of champions: Rick Mackey, son of 1978 champion Dick Mackey, wins the Iditarod. (Both men were wearing bib No. 13 in their respective races.)

1985 Largest number of foreign countries represented in a single year to date: Australia, England, France, Germany, Italy and Japan

1985 First woman to win the Iditarod: Libby Riddles

1988 First musher to win three years in a row: Susan Butcher

1989 Champion Joe Runyon conquers the Iditarod to complete the Triple Crown of mushing, having already won the Yukon Quest in 1985 and the Alpirod in 1988.

1990 Oldest musher to finish: Col. Norman Vaughan, 84

1991 First five-time champion: Rick Swenson

1995 First non-Alaskan to win: Doug Swingley

1995 Farthest run before scratching: Andy Sterns (Stopped between Safety and Nome when he feared one of his

The fastest musher in Iditarod history, Martin Buser, celebrates with lead dogs Bronson and Kira at the 2002 finish line.
© 2006 Jeff Schultz / AlaskaStock.com

dogs would perish from hyperthermia; accepted a ride less than two miles from finish line.)

2000 First year to pay prize money to the top 30 finishers

2001 First year in which three generations of Alaskan mushers competed: Dan Seavey, Mitch Seavey, and Danny Seavey

2002 Fastest musher and his Golden Harness winner: Martin Buser and Bronson, 8 days, 22 hours, 46 minutes, 2 seconds

2002 Fastest Red Lantern musher: David Straub, 14 days, 5 hours, 38 minutes, 12 seconds

2003 First musher from a foreign country to win: Robert Sørlie of Norway

2003 Largest number of scratches: 20

2004 Largest starting field: 87

2004 Largest finishing field: 77

2005 Youngest musher to compete: Dallas Seavey, who turned 18 on March 4, 2005, one day before the race start. He had placed 3rd in the Junior Iditarod that same year— the only musher to run both races in the same year.

2006 First legally blind musher to finish the race: Rachael Scdoris of Bend, Oregon

2006 Oldest musher to win: Jeff King, 50

TEN FASTEST FINISHERS IN IDITAROD HISTORY

YEAR	MUSHER	HOMETOWN	D/H/M/S	CASH PRIZE
2002	Martin Buser	Big Lake, AK	08:22:46:02	$62,857
2000	Doug Swingley	Lincoln, MT	09:00:58:06	$60,000
1995	Doug Swingley	Simms, MT	09:02:42:19	$52,500
1996	Jeff King	Denali Park, AK	09:05:43:00	$50,000
1998	Jeff King	Denali Park, AK	09:05:52:26	$51,000
1997	Martin Buser	Big Lake, AK	09:08:30:45	$50,000
2004	Mitch Seavey	Seward, AK	09:12:20:22	$69,000
1999	Doug Swingley	Lincoln, MT	09:14:31:07	$60,000
2003	Robert Sørlie	Norway	09:15:47:36	$68,571

FIVE SLOWEST FINISHERS IN IDITAROD HISTORY

YEAR	MUSHER	HOMETOWN	D/H/M/S	CASH PRIZE
1973	John Schultz	Delta Junction, AK	32:05:09:01	$0
1975	Steve Fee	Anchorage, AK	29:08:37:13	$0
1974	Red Fox Olson	Fairbanks, AK	29:06:36:19	$0
1982	Ralph Bradley	Girdwood, AK	26:13:59:59	$0
1976	Dennis Corrington	Anchorage, AK	26:08:42:51	$0

RED LANTERN

A red lantern hangs on the burled arch at the Nome finish line and remains lit until the last finisher crosses the line. This tradition of "leaving the light on for you" has been around as long as the Iditarod has. The last-place finishers award has been presented since 1973, when John Schultz, the slowest man in Iditarod history, took more than 32 days to finish the race. The Red Lantern Award winner for 2006 was Glenn Lockwood, who finished in 15 days, 18 hours, 8 minutes, and 56 seconds.

RESTART

(See also: Starting Line)

One day after the teams mush from Anchorage to Wasilla, the race is restarted in Wasilla, and the official clock begins running at the restart on the first Sunday in March. Teams leave the Wasilla starting line at two-minute intervals, and the time difference is adjusted during the 24-hour mandatory stop. No time is kept between Anchorage and Wasilla.

In some years, such as in 2005 and again in '06, poor weather conditions around Wasilla forced the restart to begin in Willow; in 2003, an unusually snow-poor year, the restart landed in Fairbanks.

RULES

(See also: Appendix I, Official Iditarod Rules)

Dog Deaths. Iditarod Rules 40 and 42 deal extensively with this sensitive issue. With more than 1,000 dogs on the trail at the start of each race, it is inevitable that dogs will die, despite the extreme care taken to ensure their health and safety.

Any health problems are usually discovered during the course of training, or at the last, the pre-race veterinary exam in which the chief veterinarian has the final decision on whether a dog will be allowed to race. But in the rare instances when a dog dies, either from an an unknown cause or from a more obvious cause, such as an encounter with a moose, the rules require the musher to transport the dog to the nearest checkpoint in the sled bag and make a complete report to a race official. He or she may be delayed up to eight hours while officials investigate the death. Follow-up steps include a necropsy and tissue examination by a board-certified pathologist. The musher may or may not continue in the race, depending on the outcome of the investigation. Race rules state, "A musher will be disqualifed if a dog dies with signs of cruel, inhumane or abusive treatment or the cause of death is heat stress, or hyperthermia."

Dropped Dogs. When a dog is injured, fatigued, or sick, a musher may "drop" it, or remove it from the team. The musher will place the dog in the sled basket for a ride to the next checkpoint, where a veterinarian can evaluate its heath. Race Rules 45 and 46 detail the

Dick Mackey held a mere one-second lead on Rick Swenson at the 1978 finish line.

© 2006 Rob Stapleton Photography / AlaskaStock.com

CLOSEST FINISH

Dick Mackey literally won by a nose in 1978, when his leader's nose crossed the finish line one second before Rick Swenson's leader. Mackey finished in 14 days, 18 hours, 52 minutes and 24 seconds. Their run down Nome's Front Street stands as one of the most stunning, unforgettable finishes in Iditarod history. The one-second loss cost Swenson $4,000. Champion Mackey won $12,000; Swenson $8,000.

Chief veterinarian Stuart
Nelson, D.V.M.
June Price

definition and handling of a dropped dog, with specifics on how dropped dogs are transported and their care requirements until they are collected by the musher or his handlers.

All of the dogs in the race are under the jurisdiction and care of the Iditarod veterinary personnel from the time they enter the staging area until up to 72 hours after the team finishes the race. Dropped dogs receive a thorough exam by a vet, and volunteers look after the dogs until they can be flown out by members of the Iditarod Air Force. Outside of Anchorage, inmates at the Eagle River Correctional Center assist by feeding and cleaning up after the animals until they can be claimed.

Drugs and Alcohol, Use by Mushers. State law applies where illegal drug use is concerned, and race rules prohibit excessive use of alcohol, according to Rule 29. Mushers may be subject to random drug testing anytime from the start until one hour after the finish.

Drug Use, on Dogs. A detailed list of prohibited drugs for dogs may be found in Rule 39. Other directives state, "No oral or topical drug which may suppress the signs of illness or injury may be used on a dog. No injectables may be used in dogs participating in the race. A musher may not inject any substance into his or her dogs. No other drugs or other artificial means may be used to drive a dog or cause a dog to perform or attempt to perform beyond its natural ability."

Equipment Required for Race.

(Also see: Section 6, Mandatory Gear, Then and Now)

According to Rule 16, a musher is required to carry specific equipment at all times, including a sleeping bag, ax, snowshoes, dog booties, a cooker with fuel and a pot, veterinary notebook and any promotional material from the ITC.

Mandatory Stops. Rule 13 states that every musher is required to take one 24-hour stop in a place of his/her choosing—whatever is best for the dogs' rest schedule. In addition, two mandatory 8-hour stops are required of all mushers: one on the Yukon River and one at White Mountain. The three mandatory stops may not be combined in any way.

Musher Conduct. Mushers must follow strict rules of conduct that are spelled out in the race rules, beginning with Rule 22. The conduct rules cover: Good Samaritan Rule; interference; food and gear at checkpoints; passing; sportsmanship; parking; accommodations; litter; use of drugs and alcohol; demand for food and shelter; outside assistance; lost food; No Man's Land; one musher per team; killing of game animals; ELTs or satellite tracking devices, and navigation.

Musher Qualifications. To compete in the Iditarod, a musher must be at least 18 years old on the race start day. A rookie musher (one who has never completed the Iditarod) must have completed two qualifying races with combined miles of at least 500, or completed one race of at least 800 miles in the previous five racing seasons plus a 300-mile race in the current or previous season. The mushers must give written proof of their standings in those races. They are then reviewed by a board for final approval. For more details, see Rule 1.

Killing of Game Animals. If a musher must kill an edible game animal (such as moose, caribou, or buffalo) to defend himself, his dogs, or property, that musher is required to gut the animal before proceeding to the next checkpoint, where he must report to an official. In such an instance, any teams that come upon a musher gutting the animal are required to stop and assist when possible. Teams may not pass until the animal has been gutted and the musher who killed the animal leaves first. For more details, see Rule 33.

Navigation. Rule 35 states that mushers must rely on old-school technology to navigate. "Mushers are restricted to the use of traditional forms of navigation. This includes time, distance as known or measured on a map, speed as is computed with simple arithmetic and direction as indicted by magnetic compass. Electronic or mechanical devices that measure speed and direction are prohibited, i.e. Loran, night vision goggles and GPS."

Outside Assistance. The musher alone is responsible for all care and feeding of the team and gear maintenance. A musher cannot accept "verbal assistance" in the form of coaching anywhere along the trail, and cannot leave the checkpoint with his or her team in another person's care. Infractions may result in a warning, a time penalty, or disqualification. For more details, see Rule 30.

Team Size. According to Iditarod Rule 17, all competing teams must be comprised of at least 12 and not more than 16 dogs at the starting line. The musher may drop tired or sick dogs during the race, but cannot add any dogs and must finish with at least five dogs on the towline.

Two-Way Communication Device, ELT, or Satellite Tracking Device. Mushers are allowed to carry a tracking device such as an ELT for emergencies, according to Rule 34, but using it is another thing. Activation may result in withdrawal from the race. Also, two-way communication devices (unless provided by the ITC) are prohibited.

SPEEDING UP

The winner of 1973 race was Dick Wilmarth of Red Devil, Alaska, who finished the inaugural Iditarod in 20 days, 49 minutes and 41 seconds.

Compare that time to the 1986 Iditarod, when 54 mushers crossed the finish line faster than Wilmarth. The only musher who did not beat Wilmarth's time was Red Lantern winner Mike Peterson of Willow, Alaska, whose time was 20 days, 13 hours, 42 minutes, 21 seconds.

Jeff King prepares
for the 2005 restart.
Sponsors' names
appear on mushers'
dog trucks, parkas,
caps, sled bags,
websites, and even
dog coats.
June Price

SPONSORS

Sponsors are critical to the survival of dog mushing and sled-dog racing. Corporations, businesses, and individuals sponsor individual mushers as well as particular races. Maintaining a kennel of racing dogs is no small commitment, not least of which is financial. Sponsors make it possible for many mushers and racers to continue.

For the 2006 Iditarod, sponsors included the following:

Presenting Sponsors: Cabela's, Wells Fargo, GCI, Anchorage Chrysler Dodge Center.

Major Sponsors: Alaska Airlines, GIT Satellite Communications, Chevron, Millennium Hotel Anchorage, Anchorage Daily News, Fred Meyer, PenAir.

Supporting Sponsors: Aeromed International, Alaskan Brewing Company, Anchorage 5th Avenue Mall, City of Nome, Coca-Cola Alaska, FIRSTRAX, Horizon Lines, Municipality of Anchorage, Northern Air Cargo, Providence Alaska Medical Center.

Sponsors: Alaska Industrial Hardware, Alaska Mining & Diving, Alaska Serigraphics, Alcan Signs, City of Wasilla, COMTEC Business Systems, Craig Taylor Equipment Co., Crowley, ExxonMobil,

Network Appliance, Nome Kennel Club, North Mail, Office Tech, Ribelin Lowell Alaska USA, Spenard Builders Supply, University of Alaska College Savings Plan.

STARTING LINE
(See also: Restart)

The main street through downtown Anchorage, Fourth Avenue is the site of the start of the race on the first Saturday of every March. Snow is trucked in to provide footing for the dogs and sleds, and crowds line the sidewalks as the teams begin the 1,049-mile race to Nome.

Aliy Zirkle leads her team to the 2005 starting line on Anchorage's Fourth Avenue. Each year, crews use heavy equipment to dump tons of extra snow on this downtown street.
June Price

The restart occurs the next day, usually in Wasilla, and mushers retain their starting numbers for leaving the chute there. The clock begins at the restart. During low snow years, the restart by necessity has been located at Willow. Once, in 2003, it was held in Fairbanks.

STRATEGY

Racing strategies are just as varied and individual as the mushers and their teams. Many mushers purposefully run behind another team, navigating by their scent. However, there are always a few drivers who choose to be the "rabbits" by getting out in front of all the other teams, hoping a storm will come between them and the rest of the teams. The downside of this strategy is that they pave the way and soften the trail for the rest of the herd. Libby Riddles employed this strategy during her win of the 1985 Iditarod.

Running grueling races such as the Iditarod and the Yukon Quest involves balancing seemingly opposing strategies. Some swear by following the competition and making your decisions based on your competitor's situations. Others insist that the key to winning is to disregard the competition, paying attention and making decisions based on your dogs only. And, of course, there is a fine line between pushing your dogs too hard, and not pushing them hard enough to let them ever fully realize their true potential.

Mushers have been known to employ tricks to mislead the competition. Some drivers are notoriously secretive about their strategies and plans. A few go as far as to provide false information to the media and other drivers. Head games do not always have to be a part of the mushing scene, though. Many regular mushers are friendly and helpful.

Planning and following cycles of run and rest may be the most difficult balancing act. Most mushers try to follow carefully pre-planned cycles of run/rest. If the driver spends too much time resting, he has no chance of winning the race, but if he does not rest enough, the driver or the team may burn out and end up scratching from the race. Martin Buser swears by his "mental-health minute," in which he stops at the team's peak to pet and talk to each individual dog. He insists that this one minute lost is worth many more gained. Most mushers take occasional stops such as these, often to snack the dogs. A common snack is frozen fish, which has the double bonus of being high in water content.

During longer rests, dogs are usually secured only by their necklines. They are rubbed down and have their booties removed. Quickly they fall asleep as their driver locates his or her supply sacks and fuel, sets up the stove, and fetches water. At checkpoints, hot water is often provided, but if the rest stop comes on the trail, the musher may have to heat it. While waiting, the musher begins to chop up frozen blocks of meat to add to the water. Commercial dry food, fat and supplements are stirred in, and then cool water is mixed in until the meal is of an acceptable temperature for the hungry team.

Some mushers choose to feed their leaders first and then work their way down the team, always patting and sweet-talking each dog while feeding it. In addition, each dog's feet are examined, and ointment and booties applied if necessary. Finally, the driver disposes of trash, returns unused fuel, eats his own meal, chats with his fellow competitors, consults with a vet, and finally falls into a brief catnap before returning to the trail. Top long-distance runners get approximately two hours of sleep per day, averaging out to a 40-minute nap at each rest stop.

2007 Wells Fargo Teacher on the Trail Kim Slade poses with a sled dog.
© 2006 Jeff Schultz / AlaskaStock.com

TEACHER ON THE TRAIL

Sponsored each year by Wells Fargo, the Teacher on the Trail program began in 1999. One teacher among hundreds of candidates is selected annually by the Iditarod Trail Committee's Education Committee. The winner follows the trail, working at checkpoints, handling sled dogs, and developing lesson plans for kids and their teachers who are watching the race daily online at www.iditarod.com.

1999	Andrea "Finney" Auf der Heyde, Bloomington, Indiana
2000	Diane Johnson, Aberdeen, South Dakota
2001	Diane Nye, Elizabeth, Colorado
2002	Kim Harrick, Eureka, Missouri
2003	Cassandra Wilson, Portland, Oregon
2004	Jeff Peterson, Golden Valley, Minnesota
2005	Lynne Gordon, Wilmington, Massachusetts
2006	Terrie Hanke, Eau Claire, Wisconsin
2007	Kim Slade, Vero Beach, Florida

TRAIL MAINTENANCE

In 1972, a race from Anchorage to Nome became more feasible when the U.S. Army reopened much of the route as a winter training exercise. Volunteer trailbreakers did the rest of the work, and the Iditarod Trail became a passable route.

Today, regular snowmachine and dog-team traffic along parts of the trail means they are open thoughout the winter, used by villagers for recreation as well as hunting, accessing traplines, and visiting neighboring villages. But other parts of the trail are opened and groomed a week or two before before the race by volunteer trailbreakers, often villagers living nearby. The trail is marked with 4-foot stakes carrying colored reflecting tape so mushers can see them in the dark in the glow of their headlamps.

During the race itself, a team of trailbreakers using special long-track snowmachines with thousand-pound sleds runs about six hours ahead of the frontrunners to keep the trail open. That means the lead mushers don't face the disadvantage of wearing out their teams by breaking trail. During bad weather, however, trail conditions can deteriorate fast, so mushers face a variety of trail conditions.

A second team of snowmachiners sweeps the trail after the mushers pass through, picking up trash and dropped equipment, and ensuring the safety of any slow-moving mushers.

VOLUNTEERS

(See also: Iditarod Trail Committee)

VETERINARIANS

In 2006, there were 37 volunteer veterinarians working for chief vet Stu Nelson. Each year they monitor the health and welfare of dogs racing in the Iditarod. Just as the dogs and mushers must meet certain qualifications, so must the vets, including five years in practice and previous experience working with racing sled dogs.

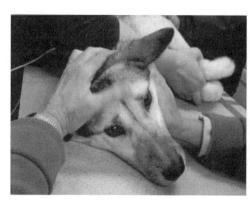

Maggie Mae, a G.B. Jones dog, gets some extra TLC during her 2005 pre-race vet check.
Donna J. Quante

Veterinarians are selected in the fall and work with the mushers as they prepare for the race, including optional kennel visits. Pre-race veterinary work includes microchipping, vaccinating, deworming, conducting pre-race veterinary physical exams within 10 days of the race start (including pre-race ECGs and blood work) and making sure each musher has completed Dog Care Agreement Forms.

During the race, the veterinarians examine each dog at each checkpoint. Mushers are required to carry dog-care diaries, which serve as written medical records for the dogs, and can be examined by vets. Vets also conduct random drug testing as a precaution, monitor dropped dog care, and determine cause of death for any dogs that die during the race.

In addition to looking out for the dogs before and during the race, many of vets conduct medical studies, including research on gastro-intestinal disorders and vitamin efficiency.

WOMEN OF THE IDITAROD

First Woman to Finish: Mary Shields of College, Alaska, with lead dog Cabbage.

First Woman to Win: Libby Riddles, of Teller, Alaska, won the race in 1985 with a time of 18:00:20:17.

First Woman to Win Multiple Championships: Susan Butcher of Manley, Alaska, who won in 1986, '87, and '88 and again in '90.

Susan Butcher gained fame for her dominance of the Iditarod through the late 1980s and early '90s. In this 2002 photo, she paused with Iditarod mascot and K-9 reporter, Zuma.
June Price

The success of these women gave rise to the popular T-shirt slogan: "Alaska: Where men are men and women win the Iditarod."

Sled-dog racing is unique in that it is one of the few sports in which men and women compete on an equal footing. While training and fitness are important, sound judgment, experience and drive tend to be the more important qualities in a musher. No women raced in the first Iditarod of 1973, but the following year, two women, Mary Shields and Lolly Medley, entered and completed the race.

Slowly, the Iditarod began increasing its popularity with women. In 1980, seven women entered the race, and all but one completed. Two years later, in 1982, Susan Butcher placed 2nd, and the following year saw an all-time high of 10 women entering the race, with only one scratch. The first woman to win the Iditarod was Libby Riddles, who won in 1985 by continuing on through a storm while all the others waited it out. Susan Butcher, after placing 2nd in 1982 and in 1984, won the Iditarod in 1986, 1987, 1988 and 1990. In the gap year—1989—she place 2nd again, just one hour behind champion Joe Runyon.

The Woman to Watch: DeeDee Jonrowe is an Iditarod veteran who has yet to win the championship, but remains an odds-on favorite of many. With an impressive record of 14 Top-10 finishes, Jonrowe is one of the toughest competitors, male or female, in the history of the race.

YUKON QUEST

The Yukon Quest International Sled Dog Race is Alaska's other long-distance sled dog race. Begun in 1984, the Quest runs between

The first running of the Yukon Quest took place in 1984, starting in Fairbanks and ending at Whitehorse. Many of the competitors have also run the Iditarod.
Yukon Quest International

Fairbanks, Alaska, and Whitehorse, Yukon, Canada, along routes historically used for mail delivery, trapping, and prospecting. The 1,000-mile race begins on the second Saturday in February, alternating the start between Fairbanks and Whitehorse every other year. Mushers finish the race in 10 to 14 days.

The Yukon Quest bills itself as "The Toughest Sled Dog Race on Earth." Checkpoints are further apart than those of the Iditarod Trail and, because the race is in February, temperatures may be colder, varying from -76° F to 32° F.

The Yukon Quest trail crosses some of the most sparsely populated and undeveloped country in North America. Hard-packed snow, rough gravel, frozen rivers, icy open water, mountainous terrain, or river flats, can make the trail fast at times or slow it to a crawl.

Although many regular Iditarod regulars also have competed in the Yukon Quest, few have attempted both races in the same year. Those who do typically use a different team of dogs. Fairbanks musher and author Brian Patrick O'Donoghue is the only person to have won the Red Lantern Award in both the Iditarod and the Yukon Quest.

For more information on the Yukon Quest, contact Yukon Quest International Sled Dog Race, P.O. Box 75015, Fairbanks, AK 99707; (907) 452-7954. Browse their website at www.yukonquest.org.

TOP 10 FINISHERS, 1973-2006

Mushers who have placed in the Top 10 standings:

Musher	Top 10 Finishes	Musher	Top 10 Finishes
Rick Swenson	24	Ramey Smyth	4
Martin Buser	16	Ken Chase	3
Susan Butcher	15	Don Honea	3
DeeDee Jonrowe	14	"Cowboy" Smith	3
Jeff King	14	Warner Vent	3
Rick Mackey	12	Robert Sørlie	3
Doug Swingley	11	Terry Adkins	3
Tim Osmar	10	Howard Albert	2
Charlie Boulding	9	Ron Aldrich	2
Vern Halter	9	Ernie Baumgartner	2
Herbert Nayokpuk	8	Guy Blankenship	2
Lavon Barve	8	Rudy Demoski	2
John Baker	8	Matt Desalernos	2
Emmitt Peters	7	Robin Jacobson	2
Joe Redington, Sr.	7	Peryll Kyzer	2
Jerry Austin	6	Joe May	2
Dick Mackey	6	Roger Nordlum	2
Bill Cotter	6	Robert Schlentner	2
Ramy Brooks	6	Dan Seavey	2
Paul Gebhardt	5	Kjetil Backen	2
Ed Iten	5	Bjornar Andersen	2
Sonny Lindner	5	Lance Mackey	2
Jerry Riley	5	Sven Engholm	1
Joe Runyan	5	Jason Barron	1
Mitch Seavey	5	David Sawatzky	1
Eep Anderson	4	Ken Anderson	1
John Cooper	4	Jon Little	1
Linwood Fiedler	4	Jessie Royer	1
Joe Garnie	4	Sonny King	1
Duane Halverson	4		

WHAT'S IN A WORD?

"Iditarod" is a Shageluk Indian word meaning *clear water*, used in the name of the Iditarod River. So says one definition. But that's not the last word. Another source claims that it's an Ingalik Indian word, "Haiditarod," meaning *distant place*. And yet another version comes from Professor James Kari of the University of Alaska Native Language Center: "The name 'Iditarod' came from an Ingalik and Holikachuk word, 'hidedhod,' for the Iditarod River. This name means *distant* or *distant place*." In 1979, Kari claimed the word was still known by the elders in the villages of Shageluk, Anvik, Grayling, and Holy Cross.

(Source: *Iditarod Silver* / Epicenter Press)

The Checkpoints

Kaltag residents await the arrival of the first musher into their village during 2006 Iditarod.

© 2006 Jeff Schultz / AlaskaStock.com

From Anchorage to Ophir, mushers essentially follow the same trail every year. However, from the ghost town of Ophir, the route splits to a Northern Route and Southern Route, which are alternately traveled in even and odd years. During even-numbered years, the race goes north, taking the mushers from Ophir through the checkpoints at Cripple, Ruby, Galena, Nulato, then on to Kaltag, where the Northern and Southern Routes converge again. On odd-numbered years, the race route goes south, passing through Iditarod, Shageluk, Anvik, Grayling and Eagle Island before reaching Kaltag.

Some of these locations are well-populated villages with the comforts of hot meals and showers, and plenty of fans standing by cheering on the mushers. In other places, such as the ghost town of Iditarod, there's not a soul around except during race days, when

NORTHERN ROUTE

Checkpoints	Miles between checkpoints	Miles from Anchorage	Miles to Nome
Anchorage to Eagle River	20	20	1,131
Eagle River to Wasilla	29	49	1,082
Wasilla to Knik	14	63	1,068
Knik to Yentna Station	52	115	1,016
Yentna Station to Skwentna	34	149	982
Skwentna to Finger Lake	45	194	937
Finger Lake to Rainy Pass	30	224	907
Rainy Pass to Rohn	48	272	859
Rohn to Nikolai	75	347	784
Nikolai to McGrath	54	401	730
McGrath to Takotna	18	419	712
Takotna to Ophir	25	444	687
Ophir to Cripple	59	503	609

Run During Even-Numbered Years: 1,112 miles

Checkpoints	Miles between checkpoints	Miles from Anchorage	Miles to Nome
Cripple			
to Ruby	112	615	497
Ruby			
to Galena	52	667	445
Galena			
to Nulato	52	719	393
Nulato			
to Kaltag	42	761	351
Kaltag			
to Unalakleet	90	851	261
Unalakleet			
to Shaktoolik	42	893	219
Shaktoolik			
to Koyuk	58	941	171
Koyuk			
to Elim	48	989	123
Elim			
to Golovin	28	1,017	95
Golovin			
to White Mountain	18	1,035	77
White Mountain			
to Safety	55	1,090	22
Safety			
to Nome	22	1,112	0

SOUTHERN ROUTE

Checkpoints	Miles between checkpoints	Miles from Anchorage	Miles to Nome
Anchorage			
to Eagle River	20	20	1,131
Eagle River			
to Wasilla	29	49	1,082
Wasilla			
to Knik	14	63	1,068
Knik			
to Yentna Station	52	115	1,016
Yentna Station			
to Skwentna	34	149	982
Skwentna			
to Finger Lake	45	194	937
Finger Lake			
to Rainy Pass	30	224	907
Rainy Pass			
to Rohn	48	272	859
Rohn			
to Nikolai	75	347	784
Nikolai			
to McGrath	54	401	730
McGrath			
to Takotna	18	419	712
Takotna			
to Ophir	25	444	687
Ophir			
to Iditarod	90	534	597

Run During Odd-Numbered Years: 1,131 miles

Checkpoints	Miles between checkpoints	Miles from Anchorage	Miles to Nome
Iditarod			
to Shageluk	65	599	532
Shageluk			
to Anvik	25	624	507
Anvik			
to Grayling	18	642	489
Grayling			
to Eagle Island	60	702	429
Eagle Island			
to Kaltag	70	772	359
Kaltag			
to Unalakleet	90	862	269
Unalakleet			
to Shaktoolik	42	902	229
Shaktoolik			
to Koyuk	58	960	171
Koyuk			
to Elim	48	1,008	123
Elim			
to Golovin	28	1,036	95
Golovin			
to White Mountain	18	1,054	77
White Mountain			
to Safety	55	1,109	22
Safety			
to Nome	22	1,131	0

Tom Knolmayer leaves the starting line in downtown Anchorage, 2005.

© 2006 Jeff Schultz / AlaskaStock.com

volunteers erect tents to house themselves for the work of the checkpoint.

At each stop, checkpoint personnel include the checker, usually a local resident who is often a musher as well. He or she records the official time and number of dogs in the team and in the baskets, and checks for required gear. Others may assist the checker, especially if the teams are closely spaced as they come into the checkpoint. At least three veterinarians are stationed at each point, and they examine each dog. Other race personnel at each checkpoint handle communications and logistics.

Anchorage

Population: 248,241 (excluding Eagle River-Chugiak)

The Iditarod makes a date with Anchorage for the first Saturday of every March, and with it comes a circus for the senses.

Snow-removal equipment operators work through Friday night in a weird change of mission. Instead of plowing the snow away, they dump tons of it onto a downtown street. Temporary fencing is installed along both sides of Fourth Avenue for many blocks. On Saturday morning there's barely room for a single file of bodies to pass through the fans stacked along the sidewalks. Coffee and hot chocolate sales are brisk, and youngsters are hawking race programs. It's bright and cold.

Mushers wear numbered bibs over heavy winter clothing. They murmur to their dogs, check gear, pause to greet friends, and pose for photos. The attention of the crowd is focused on the starting line beneath a fancy banner. Every two minutes, a team advances to the line, dogs straining against their handlers, the musher riding the brake. Stopped on the mark, with handlers gripping their harnesses, a few dogs look back as if to ask, "What's the hold-up? Let's go."

The announcer begins the countdown from ten and the musher, who's been assuring the team with touches and encouraging words, pats the leaders once more, then lopes back to the sled. At "three-two-ONE!" the dogs, like unbound springs, lunge forward.

Away they run down a corridor between storefronts and packed sidewalks, amid shouts of encouragement, crystallized breath, and thudding applause of mitted hands. Taking long, powerful strides, the dogs seem to fly along the main street of Alaska's biggest city, where almost half the state's population lives, and where—as in the Iditarod itself—the civilized and the wild have made an uneasy alliance. Running on instinct and desire, they begin the 1,100-mile journey to Nome.

Eagle River / Chugiak

Population: 30,000

Miles from Anchorage: 20

Pockets of Iditarod fans station themselves along the "urban" trail between Anchorage and the nearby town of Eagle River. Even drivers on the four-lane Glenn Highway can follow the action from their car windows as northbound mushers edge along the foothills of the Chugach Range.

At Eagle River, the mushers are met by members of their support crews. Teams are unharnessed and loaded into dog trucks for the drive to the next stop, thus avoiding open water on the Knik River and the often-snowless area called the Palmer Flats.

Wasilla (wah-SILL-a)
Population: 6,413
Miles from Eagle River: 29

After the ceremonial start on Anchorage's Fourth Avenue on the first Saturday in March, the mushers queue up again for the restart in Wasilla. The official clock starts ticking when they leave the starting line on the old Wasilla runway. Traveling along the edge of Knik-Goose Bay Road, the teams follow a trail frequently used by valley snowmachiners. Locals haul barbecue grills and lawn chairs to the ends of their driveways, forming mini cheering squads that are so close to the trail they can offer passing mushers a "low five." At these parties, ice chests are used not to chill the beer and soda, but to keep the drinks from freezing.

Knik (kuh-NICK)
Population: 10,271 (includes Fairview)
Miles from Wasilla: 14

On their way to Knik, teams pass a massive log building that houses the Iditarod headquarters and museum. The Mushers Hall of Fame is also located in Knik, which is home to many notable mushers. Here is where "Father of the Iditarod" Joe Redington lived for most of his adult life with his wife, Vi.

From Knik, the mushers leave the road system for good as the trail winds through the Bush on its way to Nome.

Yentna (YENT-na)
Population: 8
Miles from Knik: 52

The Yentna Station Roadhouse is located on a switchback of the Yentna River called the Big Bend. Owned and operated by the Dan and Jean Gabryszak family, who also serve as checkpoint volunteers some years for shorter qualifying races, the Alaska Ultra-Sport, the Iditasport, the Junior Iditarod and the Iron Dog.

For the Iditarod, Jean Gabryszak and her helpers offer free spaghetti dinners to the mushers in exchange for their autographs on posters that go to the volunteers.

Volunteer vet checks the dogs at Skwentna, 2004 Iditarod.
Heather Resz

Skwentna (SKWENT-na)
Population: 75
Miles from Yentna Station: 34

This checkpoint is located at the confluence of the Yentna and Skwentna Rivers, where longtime volunteers Norma and Joe Delia head an army of two dozen local volunteers. Some years, the couple has served meals to more than 400 people in the space of a few days. The race route follows Joe Delia's trapline route for a ways through this area.

Finger Lake
Population: 2
Miles from Skwentna: 45

Gene and June Leonard manned the Finger Lake checkpoint from their cabin there when the race first came through in 1973, and Gene entered the race four times himself, finishing twice. More recently, the Winterlake Lodge handles the Finger Lake checkpoint activity. In the 2006 Communications Handbook, organizers let volunteers know that while they are living and working out of tents on the lake, they'll be eating like kings. Nearby Winterlake Lodge chef Kirsten Dixon "prepares the greatest meals on earth."

The trail through this area is steep and treacherous, winding through heavy timber and sidehills for the climb to the pass.

Ed Iten rests in his sled at the Rainy Pass checkpoint in the 2005 Iditarod.

MOUNTAINS & RIVERS

The highest place on the Iditarod Trail is Rainy Pass, at 3,160 feet. At this point the mushers cross over the Alaska Range, Alaska's southern range that spans much of the state in an east-west curving arc. Between Nikolai and Ophir mushers traverse the Kuskokwim Mountains. On the Southern Route, they are in the Nulato Hills between Anvik and Kaltag, where the Southern and Northern Routes converge. After Kaltag, they cross the Nulato Hills en route to Unalakleet.

The Iditarod Trail also crosses two major rivers. Mushers encounter the upper reaches of the frozen Kuskokwim after the McGrath checkpoint. When the race follows the Southern Route, the mushers reach the Yukon River at Anvik.

Smaller rivers and streams are common along the trail. In March these are frozen, however, and running water under the ice sometimes overflows, causing treacherous patches of overflow ice.

Rainy Pass

Population: 2

Miles from Finger Lake: 30

When mushers leave the Finger Lake checkpoint, they travel uphill for miles to Rainy Pass, where they cross the highest point on the trail at 3,160 feet. The trail in this area is very narrow and winding.

Once over the summit, the mushers head downhill through Dalzell Gorge, which has been described as "probably the most singularly terrifying thin on the whole race."

The lodge at Rainy Pass is situated at 1,800 feet elevation, several miles below the actual pass.

Rohn (rone)

Population: 0

Miles from Rainy Pass: 48

The Rohn checkpoint consists of a lone cabin near the confluence of the Kuskokwim River's South Fork and the Tatina River. Many people consider it the most scenic checkpoint on the trail. A roadhouse once stood there to serve the dog-mushing mail carriers and other travelers on the original Iditarod Trail. That building is gone now and the cabin stands in its place.

Volunteer chops wood at the Rohn roadhouse in preparation for the 2006 Iditarod.
Jasper Bond

Built in the 1930s as a Civilian Conservation Corps project, the cabin is listed on the National Register of Historic Places. It is managed by the Bureau of Land Management, which in August 2005 replaced rotting foundation logs and improved drainage around the cabin.

About twenty miles below Rohn, the mushers arrive at the infamous Farewell Burn. In 1977, thousands of acres burned in the Bear Creek fire, and the resulting deadfall, coupled with low snowfall, makes for a bumpy, sled-shredding ride.

Jan Newton, the "pie lady" who makes it happen at the Takotna checkpoint, takes a break during the chaos.
© 2006 Jeff Schultz / AlaskaStock.com

Nikolai (NICK-o-lie)

Population: 109

Miles from Rohn: 75

Nikolai, with its unsurpassed view of the back side of Mount McKinley just a hundred miles to the east, is the first of the Alaska Native villages that mushers will pass through. More than 80 percent of the residents are Athabascan Indians. Nikolai has a health clinic, a lodge, St. Nicholas Russian Orthodox Church, as well as the city building, where radio volunteers and race veterinarians set up shop.

McGrath

Population: 347

Miles from Nikolai: 54

At the confluence of the Kuskokwim and Takotna Rivers, McGrath may not be accessible by road, but it's a regional hub with stores, restaurants, a bar or two, and a full-service airport. Many mushers take their mandatory 24-hour layover here and experience the luxury of a hot shower.

Takotna (tuh-COT-na)

Population: 39

Miles from McGrath: 18

Above the banks of the Takotna River, this village is an important refueling stop for mushers, thanks to the volunteers and villagers who offer sumptuous meals. Mushers, pilots, and journalists are fed like kings with stacks of hot cakes, breakfast meats, burgers, crab, steak, turkey, and the longtime favorites that are always on the stove: moose stew and chili.

Takotna's community building is the center of hospitality, and the whole village gets involved organizing and helping with the mushers' supplies as they are shipped in before the race passes through—dog food, stove fuel, straw, pails, disposable dishes and more.

Ophir (OH-fur)
Population: 0
Miles from Takotna: 25

Today just one cabin stands at Ophir, a ghost town founded on the Innoko River in 1908 after the discovery of gold nearby. Its name stems from a biblical reference to the source of King Solomon's gold. At its peak population in 1910, there were 122 miners in residence.

From Ophir, the race route splits. On even-numbered years, it follows the Northern Route to Cripple. On odd-numbered years, the trail wends south to Iditarod.

THE NORTHERN ROUTE

Cripple
Population: 0
Miles from Ophir: 59

The Cripple checkpoint is merely a tent on the Innoko River, the broken-down remains of what was a small settlement. The temperature can range from 10° F to -55° F. The first musher there receives the GCI Dorothy G. Page Halfway Award of $3,000 in gold. The musher's name is added to the perpetual trophy, which remains year-round at Iditarod Headquarters in Wasilla.

Jules and Leslie Mead, one-time operators of Teeland's Country Store in Wasilla, hosted this checkpoint from 1978 to 1984 when a small T-shaped cabin was still standing. Their custom was to feed the mushers first-class meals at no charge when they stopped at

Ed Hartman, Jim Paulus, Jon Rickert, the volunteers who built the bunkhouses and the entire "village" of Cripple, pose for a photo outside of their town.
© 2006 Jeff Schultz / AlaskaStock.com

the cabin. Although that small cabin is now gone, Iditarod fans well remember the thrilling climax of the 1978 race, when Dick Mackey beat Rick Swenson by the nose of his lead dog—a split-second victory that might have turned out otherwise if not for a leisurely breakfast at Cripple.

Ruby

Population: 185

Miles from Cripple: 112

The first musher to reach Ruby receives a seven-course gourmet meal prepared by the chef from the Millennium Hotel Anchorage. And along with the dinner comes $3,500 in cash for the First Musher to the Yukon Award.

Ruby is located along the Yukon River at its junction with the Melozitna River. Founded in 1911 when a minor gold rush occurred, its population boomed to more than a thousand. But since the 1920s, fewer than 200 people, mostly Athabascans, have lived there year-round.

Galena (guh-LEEN-uh)

Population: 654

Miles from Ruby: 52

Galena is the hometown of 1974 champion Carl Huntington. Also, until his death in 1999, this was the home of Edgar Nollner, the last surviving diphtheria serum run musher. Nollner's granddaughter, Rose Yaeger-Lund, organized the Galena checkpoint for the Iditarod from 1973 to 1990, when she moved away.

THE BURLED ARCH

Ruby musher Emmitt Peters was the first of thousands of mushers to welcome the sight of the burled arch on Front Street in Nome at the official end of the 3rd Iditarod Trail Sled Dog Race in 1975. But in 1999, after 25 years of greeting tired mushers and teams, the historic arch broke in pieces when city crews were moving it to the spot next to city hall where it serves a tourist attraction the rest of the year.

The first arch was carved by Red Fox Olson, the Red Lantern Award winner of the second race in 1974. That year the finish line was marked with a sprinkling from a packet of Kool-Aid. When Olson and Joel Kottke crossed the finish line, they each had a paper plate stuck on a trail marker. Kottke's said "The" and Olson's said "End."

"It was sort of symbolic of the fact there wasn't much of a finish line," said Nome Mayor Leo Rasmussen.

When the Iditarod Trail Committee decided to replace the arch, word went out across the state. Before long, logger Jim Skogstand contacted the committee saying he had a beautiful burled spruce tree on his property in Hope that he would be willing to donate.

Bob Kuiper of Alaska Wildwoods in Sterling volunteered to carve a 28-foot section of the log into a new arch in time for the 2000 Iditarod. The new arch has more than 50 burls of all shapes and sizes. Weaver Brothers volunteered to transport the carving from Sterling to Anchorage, where it was to be picked up by Northern Air Cargo for shipment on to Nome. (Source: *Peninsula Clarion*/Heather A. Resz)

Nulato (noo-LA-toh)

Population: 310

Miles from Galena: 52

Nulato was a trading site for Athabascans and Kobuk-area Iñupiats well before the Russian trader Malakov established a trading post there in 1839. Within 50 years, miners swarmed the area and the Catholic mission was well established. By the turn of the century, through steamboat traffic and contact with other outsiders, nearly one-third of the Natives died during a measles epidemic.

In modern-day Nulato, residents work at commercial fishing, local government, the school, clinic, store, fire-fighting and construction. Nearly all of the people are Athabascan and practice subsistence hunting and fishing to sustain their families.

Kaltag (KAL-tag)

Population: 227

Miles from Eagle Island on Southern Route: 70

Miles from Nulato on Northern Route: 42

At Kaltag, the Southern and Northern Routes converge, so the mushers pass through the village every year. Kaltag was the home of the late Edgar Kalland, one of the famed Serum Run mushers, and it's the last Athabascan Indian village before mushers cross an invisible boundary into Iñupiat Eskimo country. From here, the trail leaves the Yukon River and heads into the Nulato Hills through Old Woman Pass to reach the Bering Sea.

THE SOUTHERN ROUTE

Iditarod (eye-DID-a-rod)

Population: 0

Miles from Ophir: 90

Rusted-out equipment and a little trapper's cabin is all that stands where once there was a bustling mining hub of 10,000 people. Between 1908 and 1925, about $35 million in gold was taken from the region, back when gold was $20 an ounce.

By 1911, Iditarod was a substantial mining town. During freeze-up, locals counted on express dog team service for transporting gold, mail, and supplies between Seward and Iditarod.

Fred Herms, Jr., Collection, UAF 1978-14-1, Archives, Alaska and Polar Regions Collections, Rasmuson Library, University of Alaska Fairbanks

To mark the halfway point on the Southern Route, sponsor GCI awards the first musher there a trophy and $3,000 in gold nuggets in honor of race cofounder Dorothy G. Page.

Checkers, vets, and other volunteers sleep in tents; in recent years, communications volunteers set up a web camera at this checkpoint.

Shageluk (SHAG-a-luck)
Population: 129
Miles from Iditarod: 65

Snug along the banks of the Innoko River, Shageluk is an Athabascan Indian community whose name means "village of the dog people." In winter, families run traplines; in summer, the villagers depend on subsistence fishing. On clear March nights, it can still get down to -20° F. Most Shageluk homes are log cabins; newer frame buildings include the school, the village store, and the "Washeteria," where everybody goes to take showers and do their laundry.

Anvik (ANN-vick)
Population: 99
Miles from Shageluk: 25

During odd-numbered years, the trail follows the Southern Route and passes through the Athabascan village of Anvik, where the first musher to arrive wins $3,500 in cash plus a fabulous meal—a seven-course gourmet spread prepared by a chef from Anchorage's Millennium Hotel. The local church bell rings when the first musher arrives in town.

Grayling
Population: 171

Miles from Anvik: 18

The Grayling checkpoint is in the old Community Center. Through this area, mushers are traveling along the Yukon River, with the prevailing wind in their faces—a grueling factor during some years.

Eagle Island
Population: 0

Miles from Grayling: 60

The first Eagle Island checkpoint cabin was once home to the Canatser family. Ralph, Helmi and their son Steve were living a 12-by-14-foot cabin there the year the race first followed the Southern Route, in 1977. These days the "new" Eagle Island checkpoint is a collection of tents.

Kaltag (KAL-tag)
Population: 227

Miles from Eagle Island: 70

From Eagle Island, the trail follows the Yukon River to Kaltag, the last of the Athabascan villages, where the Northern and Southern Routes rejoin.

Unalakleet (YOU-na-la-kleet)
Population: 710

Miles from Kaltag: 90

The Wells Fargo Gold Coast Award, a trophy and $2,500 in gold nuggets, is waiting for the first musher to reach Unalakleet, the largest community between Wasilla and Nome. The village is the first checkpoint along the coast, and sudden storms off the Bering Sea can be brutal. Villagers are sure to offer a warm welcome, though. Kids are let out of school and the entire town turns out to welcome the mushers.

2006 Iditarod Air
Force pilot Bob
Elliot comes in
over frozen
Norton Sound to
land at
Unalakleet.
© 2006 Jeff Schultz /
AlaskaStock.com

Unalakleet is an Iñupiat Eskimo word meaning "where the east wind blows." Drifting snow here can reach the rooftops. At this point, mushers may choose to exchange their freighting sleds for lighter-weight racing sleds. It's the last of the soft snow; from here out, the landscape is windblown.

Shaktoolik (shak-TOO-lick)

Population: 224

Miles from Unalakleet: 42

From Shaktoolik, mushers have five more checkpoints before Nome. Villagers there enjoy predicting who will get to Nome first — studying the ways the dogs and the mushers look as they arrive in the village.

Koyuk (COY-uck)

Population: 350

Miles from Shaktoolik: 58

At the head of Norton Sound, Koyuk is the northernmost checkpoint at just shy of 65 degrees north. From Shaktoolik on their way to Koyuk, mushers cross the frozen sea ice on a trail that's all but invisible during snowstorms. Orange-topped trail markers and surveyor's flagging are all that guide the racers.

2006 musher John Baker slides into the White Mountain checkpoint on the Fish River.

© 2006 Jeff Schultz / AlaskaStock.com

Elim (EE-lum)

Population: 302

Miles from Koyuk: 48

On the coast of the Bering Sea, the trail into and out of Elim guides mushers through windswept territory. Local people are poised to watch out for travelers and, if necessary, will find lost mushers and get them back on the trail.

Some mushers report seeing ghost lights along the trail in this area, mostly near the old settlements along the coast.

Golovin (GOL-uh-vin)

Population: 150

Miles from Elim: 28

As the mushers come into this village, they are nearing the home stretch of the race, with only two additional checkpoints before reaching Nome: White Mountain and Safety.

White Mountain

Population: 224

Miles from Golovin: 18

At this checkpoint—with only one more, Safety, before reaching Nome—mushers are required to take an eight-hour layover. Usually, the first musher to White Mountain goes on to win. "They just take off right on the button after they take their eight hours," says race volunteer and lifelong White Mountain resident Howard Lincoln. "They don't even wait a minute."

Safety

Population: 0

Miles from White Mountain: 55

Mushers follow the shore of Norton Sound to Safety, the final checkpoint before Nome. At Safety, the checkpoint building provides the only light for miles. According to Nome mayor Leo Rasmussen, the checkpoint building had a previous life in Nome, where in the late 1930s it was a motion picture theater known as the "Nomerama." A half-century later, it was cut into sections and rebuilt at Safety.

The place was so named because of its natural harbor, known for protecting ships. From Safety, mushers must wear their numbered bibs for the final leg of the journey.

Nome

Population: 3,508

Miles from Safety: 22

Everybody's invited to join the frenzy on Front Street. Spectators line the street, flush with celebratory spirits and biting cold. The

A well-deserved nap at the end of the trail.
June Price

burled arch marking the finish line is in place. A platform stands ready to host post-race interviews and picture-taking sessions of the champion and the leaders draped in yellow roses. Whenever the siren sounds, people come rushing to meet the next musher into town. The Awards Banquet draws crowds of participants as well as spectators for a feast and delivery of numerous awards.

Nome stays on alert until the last of the mushers appears to turn off the flame in the Red Lantern. Then a team of "trail sweeps" arrives with garbage bags full of dog booties and other debris they've picked up along the trail. Nome then winds down until another year brings the mushers—and the excitement—to town once again.

Dogs and Training

Iditarod
2005 print,
"Run/Rest
Schedule"
Jon Van Zyle

The business of breeding and training sled dogs has reached a level of professionalism that the early-day mushers likely never dreamed of. Good breeding does not always produce a champion sled dog, however. The dogs that compete in the Iditarod are natural-born runners, but they also undergo extensive training, beginning in puppyhood. And a dog's individual personality also determines what kind of a team player he'll be. In those early days of training, mushers and their handlers identify traits—physical, mental, and in temperament—that indicate a dog's ability for distance racing.

To run the Iditarod, excellent health is paramount. Iditarod mushers choose a maximum of 20 dogs for screening in the pre-race veterinary exam. The paper trail for each dog includes a pre-race exam form (including proof of vaccination, blood tests, EKGs), a microchip identification sheet, verification of deworming, and a signed form from the vet who performs the exam. At this point, the

Karen Ramstead's team of Siberian huskies negotiates a fast corner on an urban trail during 2006 Iditarod start in Anchorage.

chief veterinarian has the authority to remove a dog that shows any indication of an abnormality that may endanger its health or life. All of the paperwork must be delivered to the ITC Headquarters by a deadline that's days before the race start.

From those 20 pre-screened dogs, the musher can then select which ones he or she will choose to run in the race.

BREEDS

Most racing sled dogs fall under the category of "Alaskan Husky," a breed not yet recognized by the American Kennel Assoc. More of a lineage than a breed, the Alaskan Husky is a mongrel that has been bred for stamina, intelligence, power and speed. It is often a mix between the Siberian Husky and other breeds. Dogs used in long-distance races tend to be larger, in some cases weighing as much as 70 pounds. Sprint dogs will almost always be in the 40-pound range.

One strain of Alaskan Husky is the Aurora Husky, developed by famous sprint racer Gareth Wright. His dogs are said to be half Siberian Husky, a quarter wolf, and a quarter Irish Setter. Other strains of Husky developed in Alaska include the Mackenzie River Husky and the Huslia Husky. Whatever one chooses to call them, the dogs are bred for endurance and speed. Many serious mushers keep their own kennels, manipulating and propagating their own unique strains of racing dog as they see fit.

More exotic breeds have been mushed in the Iditarod, however. One musher used to race a team of standard poodles. These days the Iditarod rules stipulate that only northern dog breeds suitable for arctic travel will be permitted to enter the race. Race officials make the final determination on what dogs qualify as a "northern breed."

Husky. Any northern-breed dog.

Indian Dog. An Alaskan Husky from an Indian village.

Malamute. Term often used by old-timers for any sled dog. Larger husky. The purebred Alaskan Malamute, however, is a breed recognized by the American Kennel Club. In AKC competitions, the dog's strapping build is judged for its traditional function as a freight dog in the Arctic, for pulling heavy loads on a sledge.

Siberian Husky. This medium-sized (average 50 pounds) northern dog is another breed recognized by the American Kennel Club. As its name implies, the Siberian Husky originated in Siberia. It was brought to Alaska in the early 1900s. Originated by the Chukchi of northeastern Asia, the Siberian Husky was bred as a sled dog, with the endurance and stamina that their semi-nomadic way of life required. Agile, fast and possessing an incredible endurance, it is a born runner. The Siberian's height is usually between 20 and 24 inches, and it usually weighs somewhere between 35 to 60 pounds. The American Kennel Club recognized the breed in 1930, leading to a split between dogs bred as show dogs, and dogs bred as sled dogs. Siberian Huskies bred for racing in Alaska in particular have been mixed with other breeds over the years producing a dog known as the Alaskan Husky, not recognized by the American Kennel Club.

COMMANDS

Sled dogs are driven not by reins, but by the spoken word. Often the musher and leader share a kind of telepathy as well. And many would rather talk to their dogs than a human any day. The Iditarod Trail Committee offers this dictionary of common words in a musher's vocabulary:

Mush! Hike! All Right! Let's Go! All are commands to start the team.

Gee. Command for right turn.

Haw. Command for left turn.

Come Gee! Come Haw! Commands for 180-degree turns in either direction.

Line Out! Command for lead dog to pull the team out straight from the sled. Used mostly while hooking dogs into team or unhooking them.

Trail! Request for right-of-way on the trail.

Whoa! Command to halt the team, accompanied by heavy pressure on the brake.

DRUG USE, Dogs

(See also: Appendix I, Rule 39)

According to the official Iditarod rules, no one may administer a drug that would suppress signs of an injury or illness, or to cause a sled dog to perform beyond its natural ability. An extensive list of prohibited drugs is listed in the rules. Also, veterinarians along the route are free to take blood or urine samples to test for drug use, and finishing dogs are monitored in Nome for up to six hours after the race, during which a veterinarian may choose to test a dog.

FAMOUS DOGS

Andy. Rick Swenson is the champion of champions in Iditarod history—as of 2006, he was still the only musher to achieve five Iditarod wins (although Martin Buser, Jeff King, and Doug Swingley would love to join that exclusive club). And the dog that led Swenson in four of those five finishes (1977, 1979, 1981 and 1982) was an outstanding dog athlete named Andy. So exceptional was Swenson's dog that upon his death, his remains were mounted and placed in a glass case. Today, visitors to the Iditarod Trail Sled Dog Race Headquarters near Wasilla, Alaska, can see Andy on

Memorial to Balto in Central Park, New York City.

Donna J. Quante

display and learn more about his amazing lifetime of adventures with Swenson.

Balto. Balto was a lead dog owned by Leonhard Seppala, the most famous of the mushers who transported life-saving diphtheria serum in the historic Nenana-to-Nome run of 1925. During that relay, musher Gunnar Kaasen borrowed Balto for his team and together they brought the serum into Nome on its final leg of the marathon effort. Balto was subsequently honored in the media, and his statue was erected in New York's Central Park. More recently, a Disney movie and many books for children remember the dog hero. Balto was professionally mounted after his death, and he is on display at the Cleveland Museum of Natural History.

Granite. When Susan Butcher's remarkable leader pulled her into Nome in first place in 1986 and 1987, number-one rival Rick Swenson sniped to the press, "When she loses that lead dog, she'll realize she's not as good as she thinks she is." Then she won again in 1988 with Granite in lead, then took second place in 1989, one hour behind winner Joe Runyon and two hours ahead of Rick.

In 1990, when Susan last won the championship, Granite was looking good for the first 200 miles until she tore a toenail and Butcher had to drop her. Two other leaders would take home the Golden Harness.

A dog like Granite doesn't come along every day. Another musher might not have seen the champion in this non-descript animal, but through consistent love and intense training, Butcher discovered and drew the best out of her leader.

The great Granite died in March 1997 at age 17.

2006 Champion Jeff
King pauses under the
burled arch with
Golden Harness winner
Salem, and handler
Lisa Frederic.
Andryce Anderson

Salem. After Jeff King took his fourth championship in 2006 (just 22 minutes ahead of Doug Swingley), he gave credit to his exemplary leader, who halted the team when it briefly got away from King outside Kaltag. In the midst of strong winds, blowing snow, and waves of drifts, Salem heard King's calls and stopped the runaway team to wait for "the boss" to catch up. King later told the *Anchorage Daily News*, "It could have cost me the race. . . . I will absolutely take luck as part of what happened. But it isn't just luck. That dog loves me, and he knew I wasn't on the sled." On his website at www.huskyhomestead.com, King ranks Salem as "one of the finest, most exciting dogs I have ever owned. . . . He is not only fast, but just plain fun to be around."

Togo. Togo was another of Leonhard Seppala's great dogs, and may have accomplished more than even Balto to help the people of Nome during the serum run of 1925. Togo led Seppala's team from Nome to Shaktoolik to Golovin, crossing the Norton Sound through gale winds and -30° F temperatures. Although Balto and Gunnar Kaasen became famous, Seppala long believed that Togo never got his due. Balto ran 53 miles, while Togo ran 260 miles. Like Balto, after Togo died, he was custom mounted and he is on display at the Iditarod Trail Sled Dog Race Headquarters near Wasilla, Alaska. He lived until age 16.

Stormy and Elmer. In lead for three of Doug Swingley's four first-place finishes (in 1999, 2000 and 2001), Stormy is an exceptional female among Swingley's "super athletes," a term he uses to characterize all of his Iditarod dogs. Swingley takes pride in his breeding and training program—he raises all of his dogs from pups. And while Stormy has been crowned with the Golden Harness three times, it was the sire of Swingley's kennel, Elmer, who got most of the praise in a 1999 *Montana Living* magazine interview. "Elmer is probably the best sled dog running the Iditarod right now," Swingley said, "and he may be one of the best ever to run the Iditarod." Elmer won the Golden Harness in 1995 and in 1999, when he ran in lead with Stormy and another Swingley star, Cola.

Bronson. With Bronson in the lead, Martin Buser streaked to a championship and a speed record in 2002, winning the race in 8 days, 22 hours, 46 minutes, and 2 seconds and taking home the Golden Harness for Bronson. "The unlikely hero" is the way Buser described his leader, who brought him into Nome again in 2003. On his website at www.aviatornet.com/buserdog/, Buser writes, "I

Zuma tolerates a visit from a Flat Stanley.
Kathy Mattes

observed that Bronson, like the previous year, seemed tireless, had a tendancy to veer left, and maintained his body weight perfectly. If one would clone a dog, Bronson might be the mold."

Zuma. The ITC headquarters mascot is Zuma, a sleek Siberian husky who is also billed as the "Famous Iditarod K-9 Mushing Reporter." Kids all over the world can log onto the Iditarod website at www.iditarod.com, and follow "Zuma's Paw Prints," as she informs youngsters about the latest race developments and other news of interest to kids. Zuma's page also includes games, facts about places along the trail, and Alaska science and natural history tidbits.

GOLDEN HARNESS AWARD WINNERS, 1973-2006

YEAR	MUSHER	LEADER(S)
1973	Dick Wilmarth	**Hotfoot**
1974	Carl Huntington	**Nugget**
1975	Emmitt Peters	**Nugget, Digger**
1976	Gerald Riley	**Puppy, Sugar**
1977	Rick Swenson	**Andy, O.B. (Old Buddy)**
1978	Dick Mackey	**Skipper, Shrew**
1979	Rick Swenson	**Andy, O.B. (Old Buddy)**
1980	Joe May	**Wilbur, Cora Gray**
1981	Rick Swenson	**Andy, Slick**
1982	Rick Swenson	**Andy**
1983	Rick Mackey	**Preacher, Jody**
1984	Dean Osmar	**Red, Bullet**
1985	Libby Riddles	**Axle, Dugan**
1986	Susan Butcher	**Granite, Mattie**
1987	Susan Butcher	**Granite, Mattie**
1988	Susan Butcher	**Granite, Tolstoi**
1989	Joe Runyan	**Rambo, Ferlin the Husky**
1990	Susan Butcher	**Sluggo, Lightning**
1991	Rick Swenson	**Goose**
1992	Martin Buser	**Tyrone, D2**
1993	Jeff King	**Herbie, Kitty**
1994	Martin Buser	**D2, Dave**
1995	Doug Swingley	**Vic, Elmer**
1996	Jeff King	**Jake, Booster**
1997	Martin Buser	**Blondie, Fearless**
1998	Jeff King	**Red, Jenna**
1999	Doug Swingley	**Stormy, Cola, Elmer**
2000	Doug Swingley	**Stormy, Cola**
2001	Doug Swingley	**Stormy, Pepi**
2002	Martin Buser	**Bronson**
2003	Robert Sørlie	**Tipp**
2004	Mitch Seavey	**Tread**
2005	Robert Sørlie	**Whitesock (Kvitsokk)**
2006	Jeff King	**Salem**

Jeff King's Tahoe may look like your average mixed-breed dog, but her champion bloodlines and training make all the difference. King writes: "Tahoe has been a beauty since she was born—perfect conformation, great coat and feet—serious attitude."
Caitlin Brady

FOOD, Dogs

Sled dogs have a very different diet than the average house dog because their nutritional requirements are so different. The average long-distance sled dog may consume more than 11,000 calories per day on the trail, compared to a diet of 2,500 calories per day back in the kennel.

On the trail, dogs are fed regular meals and intermittent snacks. Full meals are usually the mushers' own personal mix, emphasizing proteins such as liver, fats, oils, and other nutrients. This food is heated before it is fed to the dogs.

Emmitt Peters of Ruby, who set a new record with his 1975 Iditarod win, said he "cooked up green fish [frozen fish], beef tallow, and rice, put it in plastic bags and froze it." This, along with "five pounds of commercial dog food and two pounds of honey" and "beaver meat and beef" fed his dogs during the length of the Iditarod.

Idiatrod musher Joe May became an advocate of fishmeal and oil in dogs' diets. Some drivers choose to add eggs to their dogs' diets because they provide necessary protein and fat. Other items added to sled dogs' diets are cream cheese, honey, brewer's yeast, bonemeal for its calcium and minerals, and cottage cheese, which is said to improve muscle tone. Fats and oils may come from corn oil, canola oil, fish oil, seal oil, vegetable oil, safflower oil, wheat germ oil, chicken, turkey, beef, beaver, seal blubber and the tallow from meat scraps.

Dogs also eat quickly during breaks between meals. In musher's terms, they "snack" the dogs. Common snacks include whitefish and water, sometimes with gelatin or canned dog food added, and salmon, whitefish, herring or other fish mixed with vegetable, corn, flax, or coconut oil.

Mushers prepare the dogs' food prior to the race, freeze it, and the ITC ships it to the checkpoints in containers weighing no more than 70 pounds.

HUSKY
(See: Breeds)

INDIAN DOG
(See: Breeds)

INJURIES, Dogs

As with any athlete in a grueling event, sled dogs can be injured. In recent years, sled-dog racing has been criticized by animal rights' organizations that claim it causes the dogs unnecessary suffering. Mushing supporters point out that with proper care and necessary precautions, sled dogs are no more prone to disease or injury than any house pet.

Among injuries that may befall a sled dog are generalized crippling, localized crippling, muscle or tendon tears, disc syndrome, cramping, dis-locations, fractures, ice balling, broken toenails, worn nails, and dehydration.

Dehydration is of special concern in distance races such as the Iditarod. Up to 60 percent of a dog's weight is water, and it is depleted by exercise. Surprisingly, the colder and windier it is, the more likely the dog is to experience dehydration. To combat this, mushers heat the dogs' water, sometimes adding meat or chicken broth. On the trail each dog will need as much as a gallon of water per day.

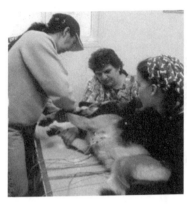

Rochester, from Gary Paulsen's team, submits to an EKG during his 2005 pre-race exam.
June Price

Dogs can lose all of their body fat and half of their protein and still function, but if they lose even 20 percent of their water, it will inevitably result in death.

Although the death of racing dogs is an uncommon tragedy—fewer than a third of 1 percent of sled dogs will die in training or competition (fewer than 1 out of 300 dogs)—various circumstances can result in a dog's death. These include gastric torsion (twisted stomach), burst blood vessels in the brain, and dehydration.

To ensure the dogs' health and wellbeing, the Iditarod requires pre-race veterinary screenings, which include urine tests for prohibited drugs. All dogs entered in the race must have current distemper, parvo, corona and rabies vaccines, and all teams must be dewormed for *Echinoccocus Multilocularis*.

Veterinary checks are also made along the trail, and mushers are required to carry a veterinarian notebook to be presented to the veterinarian at each checkpoint.

MALAMUTE

(See: Breeds)

MICROCHIPPING

The practice of injecting a tiny microchip under the skin of a family pet has become more routine, so should the animal become

The Alaskan Malamute, an AKC recognized breed, is bigger, heavier and stockier than the average Iditarod husky mix, better suited to pulling heavy loads than running fast over long distances.
Tricia Brown

lost, the owner can be found easily. For the Iditarod, that same technology of electronic tagging is useful for identifying dogs and making certain that no dogs are switched, deliberately or accidentally.

Iditarod race rules require all dogs to be microchipped and registered by a veterinarian prior to running the race. If a dog has not already been microchipped, it will be at pre-race veterinary check-up.

RACE CATEGORIES

Sprint races vary in length and usually are run in heats over two or three days. There are hundreds of sprint races, in Alaska and elsewhere around the world. Top sprint races in Alaska are the Fur Rendezvous World Championship in Anchorage each February, and the Open North American Championship in Fairbanks, held each March.

Middle-distance races usually exceed 100 miles, and as much as 300 to 500 miles. There are a growing number of these races; an example is the Kuskokwim 300 in Bethel, Alaska, held in mid-January.

Long-distance or endurance races cover more than 500 miles, and include the the Yukon Quest between Fairbanks and Whitehorse, British Columbia, Canada, each February, and the Iditarod Trail Sled Dog Race from Anchorage to Nome each March.

Perry Solmonson's team leaves the 2005 restart, fresh and ready to go.

© 2006 Jeff Schultz / AlaskaStock.com

SIBERIAN HUSKY

(See: Breeds)

TEAM POSITIONS

Lead dog, or Leader. Dog who runs in front of the others. Generally must be both intelligent and fast.

Double Lead. Two dogs positioned side by side in lead.

Swing Dog or Dogs. Dog that runs directly behind the leader. Further identified as right or left swing depending on which side of the towline it's placed. His job is to help "swing" the team in the turns or curves.

Team Dog. Any dog other than the leader, wheel dogs, or swing dogs.

Wheel Dogs, or Wheelers. Dogs placed directly in front of the sled. Their job is to pull the sled out and around corners or trees.

TEAM SIZE

(Also see: Appendix I, Rule 17)

Iditarod rules state that all teams must include at least 12 and not more than 16 dogs at the starting line. The musher may drop tired or sick dogs during the race, but cannot add any dogs and must finish with at least five dogs on the towline.

At Jeff King's Goose Lake Kennel near Denali Park, the dogs train with an innovative training wheel-and-doghouse combination.
Matthew Brossart

TRAINING SCHEDULE

Although each musher uses different techniques for training his or her team, based on experience, finances, location, and size of kennel, most training regimens follow a similar seasonal cycle.

Late spring and summer are the musher's and team's resting periods, also called the off-season. Training gets more intense throughout the autumn and winter, peaking during the racing season in the winter and early spring.

Summer. During the warm temperatures, dogs at large kennels are often exercised on a dog walker or exercise wheel. Attached to an overhead fan-like paddle, the dogs run in circles for 45 minutes at a time. This allows the trainer to determine which of the dogs have the fastest and smoothest gait, as well as keeping the animals in shape for the upcoming racing season. Another low-impact summertime exercise is swimming, which minimizes the risk of the dogs overheating while keeping them clean and cool.

Puppies are often born during the summer, so those months are usually filled with the socialization of puppies. Trainers try to handle the pups' feet frequently so that they will get used to having booties put on and taken off. The trainer also tries to encourage good eating habits from a young age. The puppies are given a relatively short time to eat before their food is removed. This process is repeated until the pups learn to eat what they are fed, when it is offered.

At eight weeks old, the pups are weaned. After that, they are taken on daily walks of 1 to 7 miles, accompanied by one or more adult dogs as role models. The walks help build the puppies' muscle tone, while allowing the trainer to see which pups show promise. Trainers look for puppies willing go anywhere: though water, over ice, across obstacles. As the puppies grow, the walks get longer. At about six to eight months old, harness training begins with ½- to 1-mile runs.

The trainer is careful never to push the puppies beyond their limits. Good sled dogs must have an innate love of the sport, and trainers never push puppies beyond what they already love and desire to do.

In August more intense training begins. Each dog goes on 3- to 4-mile runs several times a week. While the ground is still dry, the dogs pull wheeled carts, or all-terrain vehicles. Yearling puppies are often paired with more experienced racing veterans, so that they might pick up positive traits and habits. Cart training builds the dogs'

GHOST TOWNS ALONG THE TRAIL

Three ghost towns lie along the Iditarod Trail: Ophir, Cripple, and Iditarod. Each was once a bustling gold mining community that saw its peak in the early part of the 20th century. At Cripple, some $35 million in gold was mined between 1908 and 1925. Ophir was named in the Bible as the lost country, the location of King Solomon's gold mines. And Iditarod was once home to more than 10,000 people who were tied in some way to gold mining. (Source: *Iditarod Silver* / Epicenter Press) muscles, thereby gradually getting them into the routine of hard work. It also allows the trainer to teach younger dogs new commands, while reminding the older dogs of commands they already know.

Fall and Winter. The length and frequency of these workouts increase throughout the fall and winter until the dogs reach their optimal physical condition. As with young puppies, the trainer is careful never to drive the dogs to the point where they lose enthusiasm for racing.

Iditarod print 2006, "Catastrophe"
Jon Van Zyle

As the dogs are trained and taught commands, usually the trainer's tone of voice is enough to encourage them to obey, but infrequently a mild spanking is administered with a small flexible object. As they are trained, the dogs must learn not to pull off the trail to lift a leg, or to sniff something interesting. They must also learn to run fast enough and keep up with the rest of the team. They must learn to keep the tugline tight and to do their fair share of the work. It is here that the musher's mantra of "the team is only as fast as its slowest dog" comes in. The trainer will not tolerate a dog disobeying a command, showing aggression to humans, or fighting with other dogs.

By December, the dogs may be running 25 to 75 miles four or five days per week. The trainer continues to evaluate the dog's performance, deciding which dogs are best for which positions, and which dogs work well together in pairs. Factors affecting pairing matches are height, weight, and gait similarities, as well as personality matches.

By observing their tails, ears, and heads, the driver can recognize which dogs are slacking off, which dogs are tired, and which dogs are under too much stress. Above all, the trainer is careful to continuously praise his team for jobs well done.

As individual race dates approach, the musher begins to take care of some administration tasks. Early in the winter, he or she begins assembling food and equipment into bundles that will be sent ahead to each individual checkpoint of mid- and long-distance races. Several weeks before the race, the driver must make the final selection of dogs that will compose the team. For teams entering the Iditarod, by this time the dogs will have completed over 2,000 miles of training, including qualifying mid-long distances races in January and February. As the weeks before the race melt away, the dogs are taken on short runs to preserve their muscle tone and to maintain their interest in racing.

As the racing season ends, trainers and drivers begin turning their attention to breeding plans.

Spring is the season for rest; soon the whole process will start all over again.

NO HYPERBOLE SPOKEN HERE

The Iditarod's slogan, "The Last Great Race®," originated when Ian Wooldridge, a sports reporter for the London Daily Mail, followed the race in 1977 and called it "the World's Last Great Adventure." The phrase evolved for a few years and is now a registered trademark of the Iditarod Trail Committee.

Gear and Mushing Terms

Rigging includes the gangline (or towline), the central rope running between the dogs and attaching to the sled. The neckline connects a dog's collar to the gangline; the tugline connects the harness to the gangline. Booties help protect the dogs' feet and are changed out at nearly every checkpoint.

© 2006 Jeff Schultz / AlaskaStock.com

BASKET

The part of the sled where the musher's mandatory gear is stowed. The heavy-duty "sled bag," custom-fitted for the basket, is used to cover the gear.

BOOTIES

(See also: Gear)

A type of sock worn to protect the dog's feet from small cuts and sores. These are made of various materials, such as denim, Polar Fleece, trigger cloth, etc., and usually held in place with Velcro fasteners. They can wear out, fall off, and get wet—all of which require replacement booties, which are part of the mandatory gear in the musher's sled.

A musher may go through more than a thousand booties during the course of the race. Since so many booties are "thrown" accidentally by the dogs, in a final sweep of the trail at the race's end, volunteers pick up hundreds of booties, along with any other trail litter.

BRAKE

The brake looks like a steel claw, and is attached to a long brace running front-to-back along the bottom of the sled. The metal prongs point down between the driver's feet. The musher can slow his or her speed by stepping on the brake, which pushes the steel claws into the snow. A long spring slightly elevates the brake when it is not in use.

Most contemporary sleds include a bar brake shaped like the letter "U." This brake doesn't have built-in prongs, but is affixed directly to the runners. Carbide points assure greater durability. In a way, the word "brake" can be considered a misnomer, as it does not actually stop the sled, but rather slows the team and signals the dogs to stop running.

BRUSHBOW

At the leading edge of the sled is the arrowhead-shaped brushbow. Serving as a bumper, the brushbow receives the brunt of impact and damage in case of a collision. Strength is crucial, so the brushbow is reinforced with a strip of wet rawhide that's wrapped around the brushbow and laced into place. Duct tape and nylon cord can serve the same purpose. Heavy plastic brushbows have become more common, as they are often broken.

CORRALLING

In 1992, a new rule prescribed that all mushers had to rest and sleep in the same area to ensure fairness. Before that time, mushers could stay with villagers in their homes and officials could not be

Teams are transported in dog boxes, then tied off to the truck as they wait for the race to begin.
June Price

sure if anyone was receiving extra assistance. In addition, "corralling" the mushers and their teams made it easier on veterinarians and other officials who sometimes had to search a village to find a certain musher and team.

DOG IN BASKET

A term that refers to a tired or injured dog that's carried in the sled, under cover, in the sled bag.

DOG BOX

Mushers build rows of compartments on their pick-up trucks for hauling dogs. Individual boxes have a door with a window, and they are usually lined with hay for bedding. Sometimes the kennel will personalize the boxes by engraving or painting the dogs' names on their doors. The musher's sled and other gear can be lashed atop the dog boxes.

DOUBLE LEAD

Refers to two dogs that lead the team side by side.

DROPPED DOG

If a dog gets tired, falls ill, or becomes injured, it is carried inside the sled bag to a checkpoint where it can be "dropped," or officially pulled from the team. There an Iditarod veterinarian closely examines the animal, then it is flown back to Anchorage by volunteers of the Iditarod Air Force.

FINISHER

The Iditarod Official Finishers Club, the IOFC, is comprised of men and women who qualify by having completed the race. Finishers receive a belt buckle acknowledging their accomplishment and join a voting body that decides on winners of several awards each year, such as the Golden Stethescope Award, the Golden Clipboard Award, the Fred Meyer Sportsmanship Award, and the Chevron Most Inspirational Musher Award.

GEAR, Required

Booties. A type of sock worn by the dogs to protect their feet from small cuts and sores when the trail is icy and rough. These are made of various materials, such as denim, Polar Fleece, trigger cloth, etc., and usually held in place with Velcro fasteners. Mushers are required to carry at least eight booties for each dog, either in the sled or in use.

Cooker. Mushers are creative and many have invented unique ways to heat water quickly and efficiently. In any case, the apparatus they use is called a cooker. It is usually comprised of a stand, a fuel source, such as the alcohol-based automotive product called "Heet," and a metal pot to hold water or snow.

Clothing. Most mushers dress in layers, beginning with light underwear which wicks moisture away from the skin while providing insulation—often polypropylene or silk. Choices for middle layers include turtlenecks, crewnecks, pullovers, button-ups, vests, sleeved shirts, bibs, and jumpsuits. Materials for this layer include wool, polypropylene, Thermax, and fleece. Bibs are an insulated pant with shoulder straps and a chest covering, commonly used by snowmachiners. One-piece jumpsuits can be opened to the waist and dropped down (often with the help of suspenders) to avoid overheating.

Smoke, dropped from Bill Borden's 2002 team, is outfitted with a coat for extra warmth as he awaits pick up in Anchorage.

June Price

The outer shell protects the musher from wind and moisture. It should be waterproof, windproof, warm, lightweight, tear-resistant, breathable, and comfortable. Outer parkas are often filled with goose down with a waterproof outer layer such as nylon laminate. These thigh-length jackets usually include pockets, freeze-resistant zippers, storm flaps, wrist cuffs, and an oversize hood with a fur ruff.

When deciding which materials to use, several considerations are important. Wool is warm, but heavy when wet. Down is light and warm, but useless when wet, and also highly flammable. Venteel is a popular, tight-woven cotton. Gortex, Thinsulate and Thermalite are all newer synthetic materials, popular because they are lightweight and windproof. Still, traditional materials are often preferred The Native Alaskan combination of animal skins and furs remains popular, as the skin protects against wind while the fur holds in heat.

Two common forms of footwear for dogsled racers are mukluks and bunny boots. Knee-high mukluks were traditionally made with hard sealskin soles and caribou fur or moosehide uppers. Without zippers or any other openings, they were lined with grass and fitted by wrapping rawhide strips around the leg from the ankle to the knee. Now they are used with a foam insert. The major drawback of mukluks is that water seeps through easily.

Bunny boots are more modern footwear, insulated with waterproof rubber and canvas. Developed by the U.S. army, their major advantage is vapor-barriers created by double-layered rubber with an insulating air pocket between layers. However, rubber prevents air circulation, and bunny boots tend to result in damp, smelly, uncomfortable feet if worn too long. This can be prevented by changing socks three or more times a day, and rubbing a dry-skin cream on the feet to prevent cracks and splits.

The musher's choice of socks depends on the choice of boots, ranging from heavy polypropylene, to thick wool to light liners.

Mushers nearly always wear either mittens or gloves, or sometimes a combination of both. For instance, mitts with fur backs and leather palms are often worn with a light glove inside. Sometimes a musher will employ a 3- to 4-layer system of gloves and mittens, with thin liner gloves of silk or poly closest to the skin, followed by a wool or chore glove over, in turn covered with overmitts of fur and synthetic open-cell foam. When it is very cold, a gauntlet extending past the elbow may be the outer layer.

Because up to 50 percent of a person's body heat is lost through the head and neck, head and face protection is crucial. Hats made of wolf, fox or beaver pelt on the outside and wool felt on the inside are common. Parkas with a fur trim around the face opening are also popular, as they create an insulated layer of air around the face. A fleece or poly cap may be worn under the parka hood. Other headgear may include a fleece facemask, a neck gaiter that can be pulled up over the chin and nose, sunglasses, headlamp, leather eye protectors, or even glacier goggles.

GEAR, Other

Every sled bag contains at least one cooler, along with bowls for the dogs and a ladle, and cooking pots, dishes, cups, and utensils for the human driver. Many also choose to keep a thermos handy. Although camping gear used to be considered a necessity, very few tents are included anymore. Rather, most mushers choose to sleep in a sleeping bag, often using a waterproof poncho as a ground cloth, or draping it overhead for moisture protection.

Spare parts may include collars and harnesses, neckline, tugline and gangline, runner plastic, and other replacement parts. Tools and equipment for repairs may include needles, dental floss, a screwdriver, wrenches, extra bolts, hooks, snaps, nuts, a hacksaw blade and extra wire.

Most mushers also carry additional personal and safety supplies, including a headlamp, chemical handwarmers, knife, a complete set of clothes in a waterproof bag, and a simple first-aid kit. Other small items may include a space blankets, flashlights, matches, a compass, heat packs, sunglasses, lip salve, energy food and a survival manual.

Most mushers bring along a few light personal items to make their adventure more comfortable and enjoyable. Common choices are a tape or CD player, iPod, and headphones, a notebook and pencil, a camera and film, and personal hygiene supplies such as soap, toothbrush and toothpaste, a comb and brush, razors and shaving supplies, and pre-moistened wipes. An extra pair of glasses or contact lenses are almost a necessity. Savvy mushers will bring a small portable alarm clock to wake them up at checkpoints before the rest of the teams. Many drivers bring postcards, musher cards, and other small items for fans and checkpoint residents.

GANGLINE, or TOWLINE

The main line running down the center of the dog team to front of the sled, the gangline (also called towline) is the heaviest, longest rope at 3/8- to 1/2-inch diameter. The number of dogs running determines the number of gangline sections. Although poly or nylon is usually used for training, Iditarod rules specify that mushers must use cable-core gangline or cable tie-out lines for each dog. Although it is stronger, the newer Kevlar cable-core ganglines are expensive and prone to kinking. They also can become heavy due to their ability to absorb moisture.

HANDLEBAR, or HANDLE BOW

The handlebar is the highest point on a sled, and looks like an inverted letter "U." The musher uses this wooden handlebar to steer, by twisting the handlebar and shifting his or her weight from side to side. The handlebar is usually wrapped with rawhide, nylon, tape, hockey tape or halibut fishing line for added grip and strength. The handlebar is also called the drive bow, the driving bow, the steering bow and the handle bow. Although its primary purpose is to provide the musher with a way of steering, handlebars also help keep tired drivers from falling off of their sleds. Sometimes mushers even tie themselves to the handlebar, and it is not uncommon for a lead dog to arrive at a checkpoint with its musher doubled over the handlebar, sound asleep.

HARNESS

Each dog wears a flat nylon collar with a large ring over which a cross-backed harness is slipped. The harness is made of lightweight, padded, 1-inch-wide nylon-webbed material, and fits around the dog's shoulders and forelegs. Designed to place the weight on the dog's shoulders and chest, the harness helps to transfer the dog's pulling power to the sled. The harness is attached to the end of the gangline by a heavy snap or carabiner placed on a metal ring or reinforced rope loop.

ICE HOOK
(See: Snow Hook)

LEAD DOG, or LEADER
(See: Team Positions)

LINE OUT!

Command for lead dog to pull the team out straight from the sled. Used mostly while hooking dogs into or out of their team positions.

NECKLINE

Line that connects dog's collar to towline and between the two collars of a double lead. The neckline keeps the dog facing forward and prevents him from straying too far from the rest of the line or from tangling with obstacles. Between 12 and 16 inches long, necklines are 1/16- to 1/4-inch diameter rope, intended to be breakable in case of an emergency.

PEDALING

A musher can assist the dogs by pedaling, or pushing the sled with one foot while the other remains on the runner.

RABBIT

(See: Strategy)

RIGGING

Collection of lines to which dogs are attached. Includes towline, tuglines and necklines.

ROOKIE

The Iditarod Trail Committee defines a rookie as "any musher that has not completed the Iditarod no matter how many times that musher may have started and had to scratch." To enter the race, a rookie must have completed two approved qualifying races with an accumulated total of at least 500 miles or must have completed one race of at least 800 miles within the last five racing seasons and a 300-mile race in either the current or previous racing season.

RUNNERS

The two bottom pieces of the sled that come in contact with the snow. They extend behind the basket for the driver to stand on. Runner bottoms are usually wood, covered with plastic or Teflon. This plastic or Teflon is usually replaced at least once during the race.

SCRATCH

To formally drop out of the race, either before it begins or along the trail.

Jeff King, second from right, is questioned about his unique aluminum sled design, which included a combination seat/ storage compartment behind the musher.
June Price

SLATS

Thin strips of wood that make up the bottom of a wooden sled basket.

SLED

The most common sled used in competition today is the basket sled, which has a gap between the runners and the sled bag, and the racing toboggan in which the bag rests directly on the runners.

Racers have nearly replaced the smaller and less sturdy basket-type sled. Comprised of a single piece of plastic, the toboggan extends from the handlebar to the brushbow and is bolted directly to the tops of the runners. This creates a lower center of gravity, making the sled less likely to tip over. The toboggan's runners are shorter than those of the basket sled, but its basket and sled bag are larger, making both sleds the same length, about 8 feet. The toboggan can carry more gear, and is helpful in inclement weather, as it can be turned over to create a sort of shelter. It usually weighs between 25 and 45 pounds.

Together, the runners and the stanchions help make up the skeleton of the sled. The runners prevent the sled from sinking into the snow. Extending up to 2 feet behind the basket, they create a place for the musher to stand. Most runners now have footpads with a nonskid surface, or 1 to 2 feet of synthetic plastic with treads. The stanchions are vertical pieces of wood that rise up from runners and form the framework upon which the rest of the sled is built. There are usually one to three stanchions per sled. They are usually bolted to the runners at intersecting points, or the runners and the stanchions are lashed together with nylon cord or babiche.

Innovative mushers such as Jeff King are continually adapting their sleds to stay lightweight, yet better meet the musher's needs, such as adding a seat. In 2006, Iditarod.com writer Andy Moderow reported that King's newest sled-with-a-seat was made from aluminum and it performed admirably for the champion. Furthermore, Moderow added, "King figured out how to heat his handlebars. Using an open flame and a wick, King had toasty hands the entire way from Anchorage to Nome. This allowed him to work quicker: Cold hands often slow mushers down, as chores requiring dexterity take longer to complete. But his system also had its dangers: At one checkpoint, King's sled caught on fire."

SLED BAG

The sled bag, resting directly upon the runners in a toboggan-style sled or on a series of slats in a basket sled, carries all of the musher's gear and equipment, and is sometimes used to transport sick or tired dogs. Made of heavy canvas or nylon, it is fastened to the basket or the runners with Velcro, buckles and/or lashing grommets. If the bag is large enough, a musher can crawl inside to seek shelter from a storm.

SNOW HOOK, or ICE HOOK

The snow hook serves as an anchor for the sled and team. The driver steps on the fishhook-like snow hook made of heavy metal, pushing it into the snow to secure the team and keep it from running away when the musher steps off the sled for a short time.

SNUB LINE

Rope attached to the sled that's used to tie the sled to a tree or other object.

STAKE

Metal or wooden post driven into the ground to which dog is tied.

STOVE UP

Injured, generally temporarily. Applies to both musher and dogs.

TETHER LINE

A long chain with shorter pieces of chain extending from it. Used to stake out a team when stakes aren't available.

TOGGLES

Small pieces of ivory or wood traditionally used by Native Alaskans to fasten tuglines to harnesses.

TOWLINE, or GANGLINE

(Also see: Gangline)

Main rope that runs forward from the sled. Generally made of polyethylene or nylon. All dogs are connected to the towline by other lines.

TUGLINE

Line that connects dog's harness to the towline, or gangline. Tuglines are usually 1/4- to 3/8-inch in diameter, and branch off from the gangline, connecting to the dog's harness at the base of the tail. They are usually 3 to 4 feet long, and attach using toggles or brass snaps. A loose tugline signals to the driver that a particular dog is not doing his fair share of the work, although a clever dog will make it appear that he is working by keeping just enough pressure on the gangline.

WHIP, or SIGNAL WHIP

Some mushers carry whips in their sleds and on occasion pull them out and crack them to spur their teams on. They are not used to strike the animals, but rather in conjunction with voice commands to urge the dogs to run faster.

MANDATORY GEAR, THEN AND NOW

1978

1. Proper cold weather sleeping bag.
2. Hand ax
3. One pair of standard snowshoes with bindings.
4. Any promotional material that the musher has been asked by the Committee to carry to Nome.
5. One day's food for each dog, with a minimum of two pounds per dog.
6. One day's food ration for each musher.
7. Two sets of booties for each dog either in the sled, or in use and in the sled.

2006

1. Proper cold weather sleeping bag weighing a minimum of 5 lbs.
2. Ax, head to weigh a minimum of 1¾ lbs., handle to be at least 22" long.
3. One pair of snowshoes with bindings, each snowshoe to be at least 252 square inches in size.
4. Any promotional material provided by the ITC.
5. Eight booties for each dog in the sled or in use.
6. One operational cooker and pot capable of boiling at least three (3) gallons of water at one time.
7. Veterinarian notebook, to be presented to the veterinarian at each checkpoint.
8. An adequate amount of fuel to bring three (3) gallons of water to a boil.

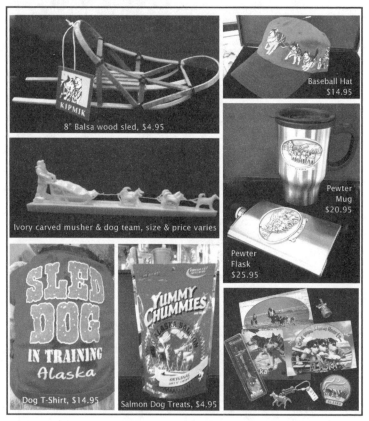

SECTION 7

Unforgettable People

ADKINS, TERRY

Veterinarian Terry Adkins was serving in the U.S. Air Force in Alaska when he volunteered to help with the first running of the Iditarod in 1973. He was the one and only veterinarian in the inaugural race. The next year he decided to get in the race himself, and then he ran, and ran some more. Ultimately, Adkins entered the race 22 times; the 2007 race will be his 23rd.

Adkins, now of Sand Coulee, Mont., is retired from the U.S. Air Force, but continues his love affair with mushing, helping novice mushers along and mushing himself from time to time. Adkins was named an Honorary Musher in the 2004 race.

AUSTIN, JERRY

Born in Seattle, Wash., Jerry Austin lives in St. Michael, Alaska. Austin is a three-time winner of the Iditarod's Sportsmanship Award (1987, 1989, 1993). He has competed in the race 19 times and finished in the Top 10 six times, with his best finish coming in 1982 when he placed 3rd. His fastest time, however, was in 1996 at 10 days, 16 hours, 38 minutes, and 40 seconds.

Though not a first-place finisher, Austin is tops in many other mushers' books. In 1989, he and some rookie mushers overtook musher Mike Madden, who was sick and delirious. Feeding him and keeping him warm didn't help, so Austin and another driver mushed to the nearest town and and returned with a helicopter that took Madden to the hospital. Austin then mushed Madden's team the 30 miles into town.

In 1993, he organized and led 17 other mushers into Nome after they were trapped by the weather in White Mountain. Austin was named to the Iditarod Hall of Fame in 1997.

Don Bowers earned the Sportsmanship Award in his 1997 Iditarod run.
© 2006 Jeff Schultz / AlaskaStock.com

BOWERS, DON

Don Bowers was a pilot, volunteer, musher, and prolific writer, who devoted himself to the Iditarod and met an untimely death in June 2000 at age 52 while flying National Park Service personnel to the base camp on Mount McKinley. His writings included a training diary, which appears on the Iditarod website (www.iditarod.com), and a comprehensive history of the trail and early dog mushing in Alaska history. His detailed trail guide continues to help rookies prepare for a trail they've only heard about, and his popular 1996 book, *Back of the Pack*, lends insight to his rookie run, his insatiable love for dogs and mushing, and the grand sweep of annual race. After serving as a volunteer pilot and attempting the race in 1995, Bowers finished the Iditarod for the first time in 1996, and in 1997, he received the Sportsmanship Award. Bowers' fastest race was in 1999, when he finished in 13 days and 16 hours.

Born in Arkansas, Bowers called Willow, Alaska, his hometown. He was an Air Force Academy graduate and held masters degrees from the Air Force Institute of Technology and Alaska Pacific University. Although he was a member of the Montana Creek Dog

Mushers Assoc., he did not race because the group was not a distance-mushing organization, however he did serve as race marshal several times. In January 2000, Bowers launched a combined 200/300-mile dog race in Willow, and he died only a few months later. Since then, the race has been renamed the Don Bowers Memorial in his honor, and it is a qualifying race for mushers in the Yukon Quest and the Iditarod. Bowers was inducted into the Iditarod Hall of Fame in 2001.

BUSER, MARTIN

Four-time winner Martin Buser, of Big Lake, Alaska, was named to the Iditarod Hall of Fame in 1998. He reached Nome first in 1992, 1994 and 1997, then broke the all-time speed record in 2002 with Bronson in lead, at 8 days, 22 hours, 46 minutes and 2 seconds. To top off that emotion-packed day, Buser paused under the burled arch in Nome to take the oath for naturalization as a U.S. citizen.

Born in Winterthur, Switzerland, Buser first got involved in sled-dog racing in Europe as a teen-ager. He came to Alaska to train with Earl and Natalie Norris and ran his first Iditarod in 1980, finishing 22nd. It wasn't long before he was back in Alaska for good, liking the wide, open spaces and sparse population. In addition to racing, his breeding kennel, Happy Trails Kennel, and talking to schoolchildren keeps him busy.

Honored for the exceptional care he gives his dogs, Buser is a four-time winner of the Leonhard Seppala Humanitarian Award. He has run the Iditarod 22 times, and his two teen-aged sons, Rohn and Nikolai, are regular competitors in the Junior Iditarod.

The State of Alaska named Buser "Alaskan of the Year" in 1995. Buser's website offers more details about his work as a breeder and musher at www.aviatornet.com/buserdog/.

BUTCHER, SUSAN

Named to the Iditarod Hall of Fame in 1997, Susan Butcher was the second woman to win the race. But coming in first in 1986 was

HONORARY MUSHERS

From the Iditarod's first run in 1973 through 1980, Leonhard Seppala, the most famous of the mushers who transported life-saving diphtheria in the historic Nenana-to-Nome run of 1925, was designated as Honorary Musher, and assigned bib No. 1. Each year since 1980, the Iditarod Trail Committee has selected one or two individuals who have made a significant contribution to the sport, even if he or she is not a musher. The first to receive the honor were the four serum runners still living in the early 1980s: Edgar Nollner, Edgar Kalland, Charlie Evans, and Billy McCarty. In 1992, the first musher racing in the Iditarod to receive the honor was named: Herbie Nayokpuk.

Year	Honorary Musher
1973 to '79	Leonhard Seppala
1980	Leonhard Seppala
	"Wild Bill" Shannon
1981	Edgar Kalland
1982	Billy McCarty
1983	Charles Evans
	Edgar Nollner
1984	Pete MacMannus
	Howard Albert
1985	William A. Egan
1986	Fred Machetanz
1987	Eva Brunell "Short" Seeley
1988	Marvin "Muktuk" Marston
1989	Otis Delvin "Del" Carter, DVM
	John Auliye

Year	Honorary Musher
1990	Victor "Duke" Kotongan
	Henry Ivanoff
1991	"Wild Bill" Shannon
	Dr. Roland "Doc" Lombard
1992	Herbie Nayokpuk
1993	Leroy Swenson
	Mike Merkling
1994	Dick Tozier
	Mike Merkling
1995	John Komok
1996	Bill Vaudrin
1997	Dorothy G. Page
1998	Joel Kottke
	Lolly Medley
1999	Violet "Vi" Redington
	George Rae
2000	Joe Redington Sr.
	Edgar Nollner
	John Schultz
2001	Dr. R. W. Van Pelt, Jr.
	Don Bowers
2002	Earl Norris
	Isaac Okleasik
2003	Howard & Julie Farley
2004	Terry Adkins
	Harry Pitka
2005	Jirdes Winther Baxter
	Larry Thompson
2006	Gene Leonard

only a beginning. She followed up that win with another in 1987, then again in 1988, then second in 1989, and first again in 1990.

Born in Cambridge, Mass. Butcher has run the race 17 times; in 15 of those races, she finished in the Top 10; in 12 races, she was in the Top 5. She was the first woman to place in the money, when she crossed the finish line at 19th in the 1978 race. Her fastest time came in 1993, at 10 days, 22 hours, 2 minutes, 40 seconds. Her fastest winning time was in 1990, 11 days, 1 hour, 53 minutes, 23 seconds. Although she retired from racing to raise two daughters, Butcher didn't drop out of the limelight. She remains a popular public speaker and operates a kennel with husband David Monson.

In late 2005, Butcher was diagnosed with leukemia, and began treatment at the Unversity of Washington Medical Center. The Blood Bank of Alaska also began the ultimately successful search for a bone marrow match among 1,000 potential doners who came forward. Thousands of cards and emails helped buoy Butcher through some of the roughest times. Having finished the first round of chemotherapy, a tired but smiling Butcher was on hand at the Ruby checkpoint in the 2006 race, working as a checker when her friend DeeDee Jonrowe arrived, and greeting many friends as she went onward to other places along the trail.

Despite her greatest efforts, Butcher succumbed to the disease on August 5, 2006. Alaskans—and fans around the world—grieved with her family.

Visit Susan Butcher's website at www.susanbutcher.com.

DELIA, JOE

Though he understands dogs and mushers, Joe Delia has never run the Iditarod. But his home in Skwenta, where he has lived for more than 50 years, has served as the Skwentna checkpoint since the first running of the race in 1973. Along with his wife, Norma, and a core crew of volunteers numbering 22, they feed and house almost 400 people each March as the mushers, the media, the race officials, and the spectators pass through. Delia helped survey the

Joe Delia with his Iditarod beagle at the Skwentna checkpoint, 2004 Iditarod.
Heather Resz

trail for the first race and served as a trailbreaker in its first few years.

Delia's own mushing consists of running to the post office and running a trapline. For years, he has put in the trail to and from his checkpoint. Delia was named to the Iditarod Hall of Fame in 1997.

DEVINE, BILL

This Alaskan artist is responsible for the design of that well-known Iditarod logo of the husky head with the capital I, a trademark of the Iditarod Trail Committee, Inc. and the race itself. In early races it was used on wood trail markers, and through the years it has appeared on patches, mugs, T-shirts, and on the Iditarod website.

Devine received 2006 Founder's Award for his work in designing the logo and in helping Joe Redington promote the race in its early days. His photograph of Redington, posing with a favorite sled-dog named Feets, was the model for a bronze sculpture that's near the entrance to the ITC headquarters near Wasilla.

HUNTINGTON, CARL

Carl Huntington is the only musher ever to win in Alaska's three biggest races of the 1970s: the Iditarod Trail Sled Dog Race (1974), the Fur Rendezvous World Championship sprint race (1973, 1977), and the North American Sled Dog Championship sprint race (1977). An Athabascan racer from the village of Galena, Huntington won the 1974 Iditarod with 11-year-old Nugget in lead, on loan from Emmitt Peters. The next year, at age 12, Nugget crossed the finish line first again, this time with Peters on the sled.

DeeDee Jonrowe is known for her focus and determination.
June Price

JONROWE, DEEDEE

DeeDee Jonrowe has finished in the Iditarod's Top 10 some 13 times, with 10 of those in consecutive years. She is the fastest female musher in Iditarod history, and she is the only musher to have competed in both the Iditarod and the Alpirod for three consecutive years: 1992, 1993 and 1994. All these and other accomplishments in dog care and sportsmanship make her a crowd favorite, and while she has finished in 2nd place on two occasions, fans are ready to see her finally achieve the Iditarod championship.

But what really sticks with the public is the way she has fought back from two debilitating events—a near-fatal auto accident and, more recently, without even taking a break from the Iditarod, she battled breast cancer in 2002. She ran again in 2003, and won the Most Inspirational Musher Award. Jonrowe remains an energetic fundraiser for the American Cancer Society and maintains a busy speaking schedule.

Born in Germany as the daughter of a military man, Jonrowe moved to Alaska as a teen-ager in 1971, when her father was transferred to Fort Richardson. She entered her first Iditarod in 1980. Jonrowe and her husband Mike operate a kennel in the Matanuska-Susitna Valley, north of Anchorage. She is a member of the Iditarod Hall of Fame. Learn more about Jonrowe at www.deejonrowe.com.

KING, JEFF

Jeff King has been dubbed the "winningest" musher, having won more than two dozen mid- and long-distance races throughout Alaska. In his first nine years of racing, Jeff King won the Iditarod three times (1993, 1996 and 1998), the Yukon Quest in 1989, and the Kuskokwim 300 four times. Since then he has continued to claim victories in every major race in Alaska. He achieved his fourth Iditarod championship in 2006.

A former Californian, King moved to Denali Park in 1975 and started mushing dogs, running a trapline and hauling freight. Soon he began entering races and discovered a love of competitive mushing. King first entered the Iditarod in 1981, when he finished 28th. It wasn't until 1991 that he ran again, and he has competed every year since then. His innovations in sled design and training, as well as his speed and dog care, have earned the respect of his peers. King and his wife, Donna, operate Goose Lake Kennel and Husky Homestead Tours from their home near Denali National Park. King was named to the Iditarod Hall of Fame in 1999. Learn more about King and the kennel at www.huskyhomestead.com.

Dick Mackey, left, and Jeff King, both history-making champions.

June Price

MACKEY, DICK

Named to the Iditarod Hall of Fame in 1997, Dick Mackey helped organize the first Iditarod and, in 1978, won the closest race ever, beating out Rick Swenson by just one second. The two teams raced down Nome's Front Street side by side, after a thousand miles of jockeying for the lead. Mackey's lead dog trotted across the line first, and even though

Mackey himself collapsed short of the line when the dogs tangled, the judges ruled that the lead dog's nose was all that counted and Mackey had won.

A tireless organizer in the early years of the race, he was also one of the most competitive, never finishing out of the Top 10 in his first five races. He has also served as race committee president, race manager, trail manager, banquet emcee, and start and finish announcer.

Born in Concord, N.H., he now lives in Nenana, Alaska. His fastest time was his winning run in 1978, 14 days, 18 hours, 52 minutes, 24 seconds. He last ran the race in 1987.

MURPHY, GEORGE

Bush pilot George Murphy has flown the Iditarod almost every year since 1980, and was chief pilot of the Iditarod Air Force in 1992.

Murphy first visited Alaska in 1959 and relocated from Braintree, Mass., to Alaska in 1965. He learned to fly, then worked as a project engineer for the Alaska Division of Aviation, helping to build airports in remote villages. Murphy, a resident of Willow, is an engineer, pilot and owner of Alaska Bush Expeditions.

NAYOKPUK, HERBIE

Herbie Nayokpuk was named to the Iditarod Hall of Fame in 1997. Known as the Shishmaref Cannonball, after his hometown on Bering Sea coast, Nayokpuk has never won the Iditarod but has finished in the Top 10 in 8 of his 11 races. In 1992, he was the first living musher chosen to be the Iditarod's honorary No. 1 musher.

He is admired as a musher's musher—respected and liked on the trail and in the dog yard. In 1983, he finished 4th, despite having had open-heart surgery five months earlier. His best finish was second, in 1980. His fastest time was in 1981, 12 days, 22 hours, 17 minutes, 45 seconds. In 1988, he was selected as Most Inspirational Musher.

Emmitt Peters and his team struggle through whiteout conditions in the 1985 Iditarod near Koyuk.

© 2006 Jeff Schultz / AlaskaStock.com

PETERS, EMMITT

Named to the Iditarod Hall of Fame in 1997, Emmitt Peters cut six full days off the race when he won in 1975, setting a speed record that stood for five years. Born in Ruby, Alaska, where he still lives, Peters grew up mushing. Instead of just camping and mushing along the Iditarod Trail, he devised strategies for resting and running—strategies that took him to Nome in record time the third year of the race. For the next five years he finished in the Top 10, earning the nickname "The Yukon River Fox."

Known for the advice and encouragement he gave to rookies, he was popular with his fellow mushers. Peters was unable to maintain his competitive edge after shattering his knee in a training accident in 1986. He has continued his involvement with the Iditarod as the checker in Ruby.

His fastest time was in 1981, 13 days, 14 hours, 14 minutes, 49 seconds. His winning time in 1975 was 14 days, 14 hours, 43 minutes.

RASMUSSEN, LEO

No history of the Iditarod could be written without giving credit to Nome businessman and Iditarod booster, Leo Rasmussen. The six-term mayor of Nome was an organizer and volunteer in the 1973 race, and though he's never competed in the race, his name is forever entwined with the Iditarod—the race as well as the historic trail. For decades, he's been at the forefront: He helped trace the old mushing routes for the Bureau of Land Management, served as president of the Iditarod National Historic Trail, Inc., sat on the Iditarod Trail Committee's board of directors (serving as president for three of those years), and worked to keep the race out of debt. Thousands of mushers have seen his face as they crossed the finish line, and today's Iditarod Executive Director Stan Hooley told the *Anchorage Daily News*, "Other than Joe Redington, Sr., I'm not sure I know of anyone who is as interested in or as passionate about the Iditarod Trail as Leo Rasmussen." He was inducted into the Iditarod Hall of Fame in 2002.

REDINGTON, VIOLET "VI"

When biographers extol the greatness of Joe Redington, Sr., "the Father of the Iditarod," they sometimes overlook his biggest supporter and partner, his wife, Vi.

Vi Redington's life story is equal to any that a Hollywood writer could conjure. Originally from Pennsylvania, she was married to Ray Redington when she arrived in Knik, Alaska, in 1948. A whole family moved up together, it seemed, including several members of an extended family that included her brother-in-law and father-in-law. Within five years, her marriage to Ray had ended, and she married his brother, Joe. Their partnership would last 46 years, until Joe's death in 1999.

Together, Joe and Vi became an unstoppable team as they worked on common goals, such as proving what sled dogs could do—whether it was through Joe's Army contracts to salvage airplanes from remote sites, or in building the world's greatest long-distance racing event. She stood behind Joe when when he mortgaged their home to ensure a purse for the first Iditarod. And she stood behind Joe when he and fellow musher Susan Butcher decided to drive dogs to the top of Mount McKinley. Vi joined Joe for President Reagan's 1981 inaugural parade, and cheered as her husband drove dogs down Pennyslvania Avenue. Everywhere he was, she was.

After Joe's death in 1999, Vi carried on as matriarch of the Redington clan, supporting the Iditarod in every way possible, and

Vi Redington and daughter-in-law, Barb, helping at the 2004 Idita-Riders' meeting.
June Price

cheering on her sons and grandsons who participated in the race. In fact, in a true Hollywood ending, Vi's death came on March 4, 2006, as her grandson Ryan Redington was preparing to leave Anchorage in the 34th running of the Iditarod. A memorial service celebrating her life was held after the completion of the race.

RECORD-BREAKERS

(See: Section 3, Records and Firsts)

RIDDLES, LIBBY

Named to the Iditarod Hall of Fame in 1997, Libby Riddles was the first woman to win the Iditarod. In 1985, she mushed out of Shaktoolik into a blizzard that had stopped every other musher. Three days later, she reached Nome, winning the race in 18 days, 20 minutes and 17 seconds.

Riddles' win captured the attention of the nation. She received a congratulatory telegram from President Ronald Reagan, *Vogue* magazine ran her photo, the Women's Sports Foundation named her Professional Sportswoman of the Year—and taxi drivers in Nome gave her free rides.

Libby Riddles would run three more races, scratching once, but never won again. Her next-best finish was 16th in 1989.

Riddles has written about her winning race with author Tim Jones, and has two children's books to her name. In summer months, she is a popular speaker for cruise ship visitors stopping at Juneau.

SEPPALA, LEONHARD

The most famous of the Serum Run mushers from 1925, Leonhard Seppala was named as the Iditarod's honorary musher each year from 1973 to 1980, and bib No. 1 was reserved for him

Seppala was one of the top racing mushers in the early part of the 20th century in a time when the top race was the All-Alaska Sweepstakes, a 408-mile race from Nome to Council and back, first run in 1908. The Sweepstakes was held ten times before World War I interrupted the annual event; Seppala was champion in 1915, 1916 and 1917. He won a number of other races in Nome and Ruby, and even won races in New England after he began racing there in 1927.

In the 1925 serum run, he mushed one of the most difficult legs, with his lead dog Togo in front of the team. Setting out from Nome, they met Henry Ivanoff near Shaktoolik, then turned around and carried the serum to Golovin, 91 miles, travelling a total distance of 260 miles. Balto, another of Seppala's dogs, was driven by another musher in the serum run, and made history for bringing the serum on its final leg into Nome.

Throughout his life, Seppala was an enthusiastic supporter of dog mushing and racing, both in Alaska and in New England, always seeking innovations in styles, techniques, equipment, breeding, and training.

He died in 1967 at the age of 90. A high school in Nome is named for Seppala.

SEPT, BOB

Veterinarian Dr. Bob Sept was named to the Iditarod Hall of Fame in 1997. He has donated hundreds of hours of veterinary care to the dogs that run the race, never entering it himself. He served as chief veterinarian in 1981 and 1982.

Sept's love of the race runs deep, leading him to take over as race president in 1983 when the Iditarod was ailing—in debt, understaffed, and overwhelmed. Sept led the race out of debt and onto a solid footing. When Libby Riddles' win in 1985 captured the attention of the nation and a broader audience than the sled-dog racing world, he was able to return to his veterinary duties, continuing to help improve the care of dogs and the rules governing their treatment.

Born in Pocatello, Idaho, he lives in Anchorage.

SWENSON, RICK

Rick Swenson is the only musher to have won the race five times, reaching Nome first in 1977, 1979, 1981, 1982 and 1991. In 1978, he missed a sixth victory by just one second when Dick Mackey's lead dog poked his nose over the finish line first.

Known for his steely determination, in 1991 he set out from White Mountain into the teeth of a blizzard that had turned back other mushers. His perseverance paid off and he claimed his fifth victory.

Swenson has finished among the Top 5 mushers 16 times. His fastest time was in 1995, 9 days, 22 hours, 32 minutes. His fastest winning time was in 1981, 12 days, 8 hours, 45 minutes, 2 seconds.

Swenson was born in Willmar, Minn., and now lives in Two Rivers, Alaska. He was named to the Iditarod Hall of Fame in 1997.

SWINGLEY, DOUG

The man from Montana, and a musher since 1989, Doug Swingley has made his mark on the Iditarod since finishing in 9th place and winning the Dorothy G. Page Halfway Award and Rookie of the Year Award in his first year. More firsts were to follow. In 1995, he became the first non-Alaskan to win the race, and sealed his place in the books with three consecutive wins in 1999, 2000 and 2001.

Doug Swingley is surrounded by young fans at the 2005 mushers' meeting.
June Price

A laid-back Swingley appeared in 2002, and he virtually mosied down the trail in would he would call his "retirement" run. After coming in 40th, Swingley married musher Melanie Shirilla under the burled arch in Nome, and the following year he did not appear at the starting line.

Retirement was brief, though, and the ever-confident Swingley came back in 2004; however, he was forced to scratch under emergency circumstances when he froze his corneas. In 2006, Swingley and King traded the lead as the two great mushers came closer to the finish line. Ultimately, Swingley's decision to rest his dogs a while longer may have cost him the championship, but he told interviewers it was the right thing for the team, regardless of the outcome.

Doug and Melanie live in Lincoln, Mont., where working dogs and horses fill their days. Read more about Swingley on his website: www.dougswingley.com.

VAUGHAN, NORMAN

Norman Vaughan first entered the Iditarod in 1975 at the age of 72, beginning a career that included four finishes out of 13 attempts. A lifelong adventurer, Vaughan lived by his motto: *Dream big and dare to fail.* He made headlines as a young man when he accompanied Admiral Richard Byrd on his 1928 expedition to the South

At age 99, Norman Vaughan was among the spectators at the 2005 Willow restart.

June Price

Pole as chief dog driver. In a life rich with achievement, Vaughan took part in President Jimmy Carter's inaugural parade, demonstrated mushing to Pope John Paul II, and in 1997, organized a race that is today known as the Norman Vaughan Serum Run 25, commemorating the mushers who helped stave off the Nome diphtheria epidemic.

In 1987, Vaughan received the Most Inspirational Musher from the Iditarod Offical Finishers Club. He died on Dec. 23, 2005, just four days after his 100th birthday. Vaughan was named Honorary Musher for the 2006 Iditarod, along with the late Mellen Shea, an Iditarod finisher and avid supporter of the Norman Vaughan Serum Run 25.

FURTHER READING
AND OTHER RESOURCES

BOOKS

For great reading about the Iditarod and sled-dog racing, look for these books from Epicenter Press (www.EpicenterPress.com):

Adventures of the Iditarod Air Force: True Stories about the Pilots who Fly for Alaska's Famous Sled Dog Race, by Ted Mattson

Father of the Iditarod: The Joe Redington Story, by Lew Freedman

Honest Dogs: A Story of Triumph & Regret from the World's Toughest Sled Dog Race, by Brian Patrick O'Donoghue

Iditarod Classics: Tales of the Trail Told by the Men and Women Who Race Across Alaska, by Lew Freedman

Iditarod Country: Exploring the Route of The Last Great Race® by Tricia Brown; photography by Jeff Schultz (out of print)

Iditarod Dreams: A Year in the Life of Alaskan Sled Dog Racer DeeDee Jonrowe, by Lew Freedman

Iditarod Silver, text by Lew Freedman; photography by Jeff Schultz (out of print)

Jon Van Zyle's Iditarod Memories: 25 Years of Poster Art from the Last Great Race, by Jon Van Zyle

One Second to Glory, by Lew Freedman

Riding the Wild Side of Denali: Alaska Adventures with Horses and Huskies, by Miki & Julie Collins

Sled Dog Wisdom, edited by Tricia Brown

Spirit of the Wind: The Story of George Attla, Alaska's Legendary Sled Dog Sprint Champ, by Lew Freedman

Other books for adults about sled-dog racing and the Iditarod include:

Adventure in Alaska, by S.A. Kramer; illustrated by Karen Meyer, Random House

Alone Across the Arctic, by Pam Flowers with Ann Dixon, Alaska Northwest Books

Back of the Pack, by Don Bowers, Publication Consultants

The Cruelest Miles: The Heroic Story of Dogs and Men in a Race against an Epidemic, by Gay Salisbury and Laney Salisbury, W. W. Norton & Co.

Dogs of the Iditarod, by Jeff Schultz, Sasquatch Books

Fan's Guide to the Iditarod, by Mary H. Hood, Alpine Publications

Following my Father's Dreams: Journals from a Rookie Iditarod Run, by James and Christopher Warren, BookSurge Publishing

Iditarod, by Shelley Gill, et al, Algonquin Books

Iditarod: The Great Race to Nome, by Bill Sherwonit; photography by Jeff Schultz, Sasquatch Books

Iditarod: Women on the Trail, by Nicki J. Nielsen, Wolfdog Publications

Iditarod Glory, by Jeff Schultz and Brian Patrick O'Donoghue, Graphic Arts Center Publishing Co.

The Joy of Running Sled Dogs, by Noel K. Flanders, Alpine Publications

The Last Great Race, by Tim Jones, Stackpole Books

No End in Sight: My Life as a Blind Iditarod Racer, by Rachael Scdoris, St. Martin's Press

Race Across Alaska, by Libby Riddles and Tim Jones, Stackpole Books

Running North, by Ann Mariah Cook, Wheeler Publishers

Running with Champions: A Midlife Journey on the Iditarod Trail, by Lisa Frederic, Alaska Northwest Books

Sled Dog Trails, by Mary Shields, Pyrola Publications

The Speed Mushing Manual, by Jim Welch, Sirius Publishing

Winning Strategies for Distance Mushers, by Joe Runyon

Winterdance: The Fine Madness of Running the Iditarod, by Gary Paulsen, Harcourt Brace

Yukon Alone, by John Balzar, Henry Holt & Co.

For children:

Akiak: A Tale from the Iditarod, by Robert J. Blake, Philomel

Balto and the Great Race, by Elizabeth Cody Kimmel, Random House Books for Young Readers

Big-Enough Anna: The Little Sled Dog who Braved the Arctic, by Pam Flowers with Ann Dixon; illustrated by Bill Farnsworth, Alaska Northwest Books

Danger the Dog Yard Cat, by Libby Riddles, Shelley Gill; illustrated by Shannon Cartwright, Paws IV Publishing

Dogteam, by Gary Paulsen, Dragonfly Books

Foxy's Tale, by Ed White and Donna Freedman, Whitehouse Publishing

The Great Serum Race: Blazing the Iditarod Trail, by Debbie Miller; illustrated by Jon Van Zyle, Walker Books for Young Readers

Kiana's Iditarod, by Shelley Gill; illustrated by Shannon Cartwright, Paws IV Publishing

Susan Butcher and the Iditarod Trail, by Ellen M. Dolan, Walker & Co. Library

Susan Butcher, Sled Dog Racer (The Achievers), by Ginger Wadsworth, Lerner Publication Company

Storm Run, by Libby Riddles; illustrated by Shannon Cartwright, Paws IV Publishing

Togo, by Robert J. Blake, Philomel

NOTE: Some titles may be out of print.

WEBSITES

Any search engine will find dozens of websites relating to the Iditarod Trail Sled Dog Race, dog mushing, Alaska, sprint racing, and other related topics. Here are a few to get your online Iditarod enjoyment started:

Alaska magazine: www.alaskamagazine.com

Alaska Public Radio Network: www.alaskaone.com/iditarod

Alaska Stock Images: www.AlaskaStock.com

Alaskan Sled Dog and Racing Assoc.: www.corecom.net

Anchorage Convention & Visitors Bureau: www.anchorage.net

Anchorage Daily News: www.adn.com

Cabela's: www.cabelas.com

Epicenter Press: www.EpicenterPress.com

Fairbanks Daily News-Miner: www.news-miner.com

The (Wasilla, AK) *Frontiersman*: www.frontiersman.com
Iditarod Trail Committee: www.iditarod.com
International Sled Dog Racing Assoc.: www.isdra.org
Jeff Schultz Photography: www.AlaskaStock.com
Jon Van Zyle Gallery: www.jonvanzyle.com
Junior Iditarod: www.jriditarod.com
Mushing magazine: www.mushing.com
Nome Convention & Visitors Bureau: www.alaska.net/~nome/
Nome Nugget: www.nomenugget.com
Sled Dog Central: www.sleddogcentral.com
Working Dog Web: www.workingdogweb.com/Iditarod.htm
Yukon Quest: www.yukonquest.org

ORGANIZATIONS

Alaska Dog Mushers' Assoc.
P.O. Box 70662
Fairbanks, AK 99707
(907) 457-MUSH
www.sleddog.org

Alaska Sled Dog and Racing Assoc.
P.O. Box 110569
Anchorage, AK 99511
Tozier Track: (907) 562-2235
www.asdra.org

Alaska Skijoring and Pulk Assoc.
P.O. Box 82843
Fairbanks, Alaska 99708
www.sleddog.org/skijor

Chugiak Dog Mushers
Chugiak, AK
(907) 689-7899
www.chugiakdogmushers.com

Copper Basin 300
P.O. Box 110
Glennallen, AK 99588
www.cb300.com

Kotzebue Dog Mushers' Assoc.
Kobuk 440
P.O. Box 964
Kotzebue, AK 99752
(907) 442-2600
www.kotzdogmushers.org

Iditarod Trail Committee
P.O. Box 870800
Wasilla, Alaska 99687
(907) 376-5155
www.iditarod.com

International Sled Dog Racing
    Assoc., Inc. (ISDRA)
P.O. Box 446
Nordman, ID 83848
www.isdra.org

Junior Iditarod
P.O. Box 870800
Wasilla, AK 99687
www.jriditarod.com

Klondike 300
Host: Big Lake "Aurora" Lions Club
P.O. Box 520048
Big Lake, Alaska 99652
www.klondike300.org

Kuskokwim 300 Race
    Committee
P.O. Box 3001
Bethel, AK 99559
(907) 543-3300
www.k300.org/bethelinfo.htm

Montana Creek Dog
    Mushers Assoc.
Don Bowers Memorial Race
P.O. Box 441
Willow, AK 99688
www.mcdma.org

Mushing magazine
P.O. Box 149
Ester, Alaska 99725
www.mushing.com

Nenana Dog Mushers' Assoc.
c/o P.O. Box 281
Nenana, Alaska 99760

Mush with P.R.I.D.E.
    (Proving Responsible
    Information on a Dog's
    Environment)
P.O. Box 84519
Fairbanks, AK 99708
www.mushwithpride.org

Team and Trail
531 Milner Drive
Red Lion, PA 17356
(717) 244-0671
www.team-and-trail.com

Yukon Quest International, Ltd.
600 Third St., #197
P.O. Box 75015
Fairbanks, AK 99707
(907) 452-7954
www.yukonquest.org

Appendix I

IDITAROD TRAIL INTERNATIONAL SLED DOG RACE

OFFICIAL 2007 RULES

Policy Preamble – The Iditarod Trail International Sled Dog Race shall be a race for all dog mushers meeting the entry qualifications as set forth by the Board of Directors of the Iditarod Trail Committee, Inc. Recognizing the varying degrees of experience, monetary support and residence locations of a musher, with due regard to the safety of mushers and the humane care and treatment of dogs, The Trail Committee shall encourage and maintain the philosophy that the race be constructed to permit all qualified mushers who wish to enter and complete the race to do so. The object of the race is to determine which musher and dogs can cover the race in the shortest time under their own power and without aid of others. That is determined by the nose of the first dog to cross the finish line. To that end, the Iditarod Trail Committee has established these rules and policies to govern the race.

Policy Intent – The intent of these rules is to ensure fair competition and the humane care of sled dogs. The race should be won or lost by the musher and dogs on merit rather than technicalities. Race officials appointed by the ITC are responsible for interpreting the rules in keeping with that intent.

PRE-RACE PROCEDURES AND ADMINISTRATIVE RULES

Rule 1 – **Musher Qualifications**: A musher is qualified to race the Iditarod if:

- He/she is 18 years of age as of the starting date of the Race;
- He/she has completed a prior Iditarod Race, or
- He/she has completed the Yukon Quest International Sled Dog Race prior to signing up or entering the Iditarod Race, or;
- For the 2007 race, after July 1, 2004, he/she has completed two approved qualifying races with an accumulated total of at least 500 miles and he/she finished in the top 75% of

the field or in an elapsed time of no more than twice the elapsed time of the race winner.

•   Mushers must be in good financial standing with the ITC prior to the mushers' meeting.

Proof of Qualification:

•   Except for a prior Iditarod, it is the musher's responsibility to provide written proof of completion of qualifiers to the Iditarod prior to February 14, 2007.

Qualifying Board:

•   All rookie musher qualifications will be reviewed by a qualifying board appointed by the ITC. The board will make recommendations to the ITC executive committee. Rookies will be notified of acceptance or rejection.

Musher Meetings:

•   Rookies must attend a rookie musher meeting the weekend of December 2, 2006, dates, time and place to be determined by the race marshal.

•   All mushers must attend the pre-race musher meeting Thursday, March 1, 2007, starting at 9:00 a.m.

•   A fine from $50 to $500 will be assessed for tardiness at either the rookie meeting or pre-race musher meeting.

Musher Draw and Starting Positions:

All mushers qualified to race must be present at the pre-race banquet on Thursday, March 1, 2007. Each musher will personally choose his/her starting position. Selections will be made in order of sign up and mushers may choose any position that has not been chosen.

Starting in 2010, all qualifiers must be completed prior to a mushers' signing up for the Race.

Rule 2 – Entries: Entries will be accepted from June 24, 2006, until December 1, 2006, by the Iditarod Trail Committee (ITC), P.O. Box 870800, Wasilla, Alaska 99687-0800. Kennels entering must indicate the musher's name with their entry. Entries may be presented to the ITC in person by the musher, or by mail.

Mushers who enter in person will sign a log indicating the date and time that they arrived at ITC Headquarters, which shall be utilized in determining the order of sign up. A musher will maintain his or her place in the sign up order so long as he or she does not leave ITC property.

Mailed entries will be recorded by postmark. Entries received with the same postmark will be recorded alphabetically for southern route races and in reverse alphabetical order for northern route races.

An entry will not be considered complete until the entry fee is paid in full, the race application is completed, signed and turned in, the participant's release is signed, notarized and turned in, and the Nome housing form is completed and turned in. The local contact form and the dog care agreement will be turned in no later than food drop.

The ITC reserves the right to reject entries not in conformance with these policies and rules or from mushers who do not exemplify the spirit and principle of the Iditarod Trail Committee as set forth in the rules, policy, bylaws and mission statement. The decision to reject any entry will be made by the executive committee. A musher may appeal such a decision to the full Board of Directors within fourteen (14) days. The decision of the full Board will be final and binding.

No one convicted of a charge of animal abuse or neglect, as such is defined under Alaska law, may enter the Iditarod Trail Sled Dog Race.

Any entry received after December 1, must be accompanied by a $1750 non-refundable fee. The qualified musher will be allowed to enter after all normal policies and procedures have been met, the normal entry fee has been received and another musher withdraws. No musher will be allowed to sign up after February 14, 2007.

Rule 3 – Entry Fee: The entry fee is $1,850.00 US, which includes Iditarod and P.R.I.D.E. membership dues and return postage, payable on or after June 24, 2006. This entry fee must be received by the ITC or postmarked by midnight, December 1, 2006. Payment of the $1,850.00 US constitutes the musher's intention to enter the race and acknowledges that the musher agrees to comply with these policies and rules.

Upon written request, mushers withdrawing from the race on or before12:00 noon, January 26, 2007, will receive a $1,500 refund of their entry fee. Upon written request, mushers withdrawing after January 26, 2006, and before the close of business on February 14, 2007, will receive a $1,000 refund of their entry fee. After February 14, 2007, no part of the entry fee will be refunded.

Entry fees received that are not in compliance with this policy shall be refunded and the musher shall not be allowed to participate.

Rule 4 – Substitutes: Substitute drivers will be allowed only in cases of emergency and only if approved by the race marshal prior to the restart of the Race.

Rule 5 – Race Start and Restart: The official starting date and time for the 2007 race will be March 3, 2007, at 10:00 a.m. in Anchorage, Alaska.

The restart will be on Sunday March 4, 2007, at 2:00 p.m. at a designated location. Teams will leave the restart line in the same order as they left Anchorage on Saturday.

The race will be held as scheduled regardless of weather conditions. The starting place and/or restarting place may be changed by the race marshal due to weather and/or trail conditions. A handler may be required at the start and/or restart at the discretion of the race marshal.

Rule 6 – Race Timing: For elapsed time purposes, the race will be a common start event. Each musher's total elapsed time will be calculated using 2:00 p.m., Sunday March 4, 2007, as the starting time. Teams will leave the start and the restart in intervals of not less than two minutes, and the time differential will be adjusted during the twenty-four (24) hour mandatory layover. No time will be kept at the Saturday event.

Late starting teams will leave in the order drawn must start two (2) minutes after the musher who drew last place has left. Succeeding late start teams will leave in succeeding order. Time differential for late starters will be calculated according to their scheduled starting time rather than the actual starting time.

At the mushers' meeting, the mushers will be given the starting and restarting intervals.

Rule 7 – Advertising, Public Relations & Publicity: The Iditarod Trail Committee has the unqualified and unrestricted authority to authorize the photographing and collecting of information about the race and all participants therein, and to use such photographs and information for its use in advertising, public relations or other publicity purposes. Each musher shall sign any and all documents as may be requested by the Iditarod Trail Committee.

Rule 8 – Media: Interviews and/or video graphic opportunities shall be granted to credentialed members of the media at the discretion of the individual musher prior to, during, and following the Race, utilizing the following as specific guidelines:

• Only the broadcast rights holder shall be granted live interviews and/or video graphic opportunities from two hours prior to the start of the Race and until one hour has elapsed following arrival in Nome.

• In the event that more than one camera crew is present in any checkpoint, the first opportunity for an interview shall be granted to the rights holder.

• No special arrangements for the carrying of the broadcasting and/or recording equipment of any sort may be made by any musher without the express written approval of the Executive Director.

• A musher will use his/her best personal effort to insure that the spirit of these guidelines is adhered to.

Alleged violation(s) will be reported to the ITC Board of Directors. Flagrant or knowing violations of these guidelines shall be subject to penalties assessed by the ITC Board of Directors including, but not limited to, disqualification and the potential forfeiture of his or her entire purse winnings.

Rule 9 – Awards Presentation: All mushers who have crossed the finish line up to two (2) hours before the awards presentation must be present and the winner must have his/her lead dog(s) present for recognition. Any musher crossing the finish line who is able to attend the awards presentation ceremony prior to its beginning, will be included in the awards presentation ceremony in the proper order. All mushers reaching the banquet before its conclusion will be introduced and given the opportunity to appear before the audience.

Rule 10 – Scratched Mushers: ITC will provide transportation to either Anchorage or Nome for any musher who scratches from the race, including his or her dogs and accompanying gear. A musher must accompany the team to a destination selected by the ITC. A $500 fine will be assessed if promotional material is not turned in.

Rule 11 – Purse: It is anticipated that a purse of approximately $794,800 be shared and that the purse will be finalized December 15, 2006. In addition, beginning with 31st place, $1,049.00 will be paid to each remaining finisher.

MUSHER CONDUCT AND COMPETITION

Rule 12 – Checkpoints: A musher must personally sign in at each checkpoint before continuing, except at the restart.

Rule 13 – Mandatory Stops: A musher must personally sign in and out to start and complete all mandatory stops.

Twenty-Four-Hour Stop: A musher must take one mandatory twenty-four (24) hour stop during the race. The twenty-four (24) hour stop may be taken at the musher's option at a time most beneficial to the dogs. The starting differential will be adjusted during each team's twenty-four (24) hour stop. It is the musher's responsibility to remain for the entire twenty-four (24) hour period plus starting differential. The ITC will give each musher the required time information prior to leaving the starting line.

Eight-Hour Mandatory Stops: In addition to the mandatory twenty-four (24) hour stop, a musher must take one eight (8) hour stop on the Yukon or Shageluk and one eight (8) hour stop at White Mountain.

None of the three (3) mandatory stops may be combined.

Rule 14 – Bib: A musher is required to carry his/her official ITC bib from the start and restart, according to direction from the race marshal at the mushers' meeting and from the White Mountain checkpoint to Safety checkpoint. The musher must wear the bib in a visible fashion from Safety Checkpoint to Nome. The winner shall continue to wear the bib through the lead dog ceremony. All promotional material, except the bib, must be returned to the ITC at the finish line, or in the case of mushers who scratch, to the official accepting the musher's scratch form.

Rule 15 – Sled: A musher has a choice of sled subject to the requirement that some type of sled or toboggan must be drawn. The sled or toboggan must be capable of hauling any injured or fatigued dogs under cover, plus equipment and food. Braking devices must be constructed to fit between the runners and not to extend beyond the tails of the runners. No more than three (3) sleds can be used by a musher during the race after the restart. No more than two (2) sleds can be shipped beyond the restart. Should a musher use another musher's sled for any reason that will be considered one (1) of the three (3) allowable sleds. These sleds may be used at the musher's discretion. Sleds or mushers may not be assisted with sails or wheels. Ski poles are allowed. No other sled exchanges are permitted except that a sled damaged beyond repair may be replaced if approved by an official. Once a sled has been left behind, it cannot be transported along the trail. It cannot be used again unless approved by the race marshal as a replacement for a broken sled.

Rule 16 – Mandatory Items: A musher must have with him/her at all times the following items:

- Proper cold weather sleeping bag weighing a minimum of 5 lbs.
- Ax, head to weigh a minimum of 1¾ lbs., handle to be at least 22" long.
- One pair of snowshoes with bindings, each snowshoe to be at least 252 square inches in size.
- Any promotional material provided by the ITC.
- Eight booties for each dog in the sled or in use.
- One operational cooker and pot capable of boiling at least three (3) gallons of water at one time.
- Veterinarian notebook, to be presented to the veterinarian at each checkpoint.
- An adequate amount of fuel to bring three (3) gallons of water to a boil.
- Cable gangline or cable tie out capable of securing dog team.

When leaving a checkpoint adequate emergency dog food must be on the sled. (This will be carried in addition to what you carry for routine feeding and snacking.)

Gear may be checked at all checkpoints except Safety.

Vet books will be checked by a veterinarian or in the absence of a veterinarian may be checked by a designated race official.

Rule 17 – Dog Maximums and Minimums: The maximum number of dogs a musher may start the race with is sixteen (16) dogs. A musher must have at least twelve (12) dogs on the line to start the race. At least five (5) dogs must be on the towline at the finish line. No dogs may be added to a team after the restart of the race. All dogs must be either on the towline or hauled in the sled and cannot be led behind the sled or allowed to run loose.

Rule 18 – Unmanageable Teams: A musher may seek the aid of others to control an unmanageable team.

Rule 19 – Driverless Team: A team and driver must complete the entire race trail including checking in at all required locations. A driverless team or loose dog may be stopped and secured by anyone. The driver may recover his/her team either on foot, with assistance from another musher or mechanized vehicle and continue the race. Motorized assistance must be reported to an official at the next checkpoint. If mechanized help is used and advantage has been gained, the race marshal may impose appropriate sanctions.

Rule 20 – Teams Tied Together: Two or more teams may not be tied together except in an emergency. Any team so involved must notify officials at the next checkpoint.

Rule 21 – Motorized Vehicles: A musher may not be accompanied by or accept assistance from any motorized vehicle that gives help to the musher, including aircraft and snow machines, except when recovering a loose dog or driverless team.

Rule 22 – Sportsmanship: Any musher must use civil conduct and act in a sportsmanlike manner throughout the race. Abusive treatment of anyone is prohibited.

Rule 23 – Good Samaritan Rule: A musher will not be penalized for aiding another musher in an emergency. Incidents must be explained to race officials at the next checkpoint.

Rule 24 – Interference: A musher may not tamper with another musher's dogs, food or gear or interfere in any manner with the progress of another team.

Rule 25 – Passing: When one team approaches within fifty (50) feet of another team, the team behind shall have the immediate right of way upon demand. The musher ahead must stop the dogs and hold them to the best of his/her ability for a maximum of one minute or until the other team has passed, whichever occurs first. The passed team must remain behind at least fifteen (15) minutes before demanding the trail.

Rule 26 – Parking: A musher must select a campsite off the race trail so that the team cannot interfere with other teams, i.e., no snacking of dogs on the trail. A musher needing to stop momentarily must not interfere with the progress of another team. Teams must be parked at checkpoints in places that do not interfere with the movements of other teams and mushers. A musher is responsible for properly securing an unattended team. No parking or camping is permitted within one (1) mile of checkpoints or villages.

Rule 27 – Accommodations: Mushers may only use officially authorized accommodations.

Accommodations and or hospitality outside checkpoints must be a) open to all race participants and, b) locations made notice of at the mushers' meeting prior to the start of the Race.

Rule 28 – Litter: No litter of any kind may be left on the trail, in camps, or in checkpoints. All material remaining in checkpoints must be left in designated areas. In localized holding area and on the trail, excessive left over dog food is considered litter. For purposes of these rules, straw is not considered litter. Straw must be removed from plastic bags before it is taken from the holding area at checkpoints.

Rule 29 – Use of Drugs and Alcohol: Drug or alcohol impairment and drug use by mushers during the Race is prohibited. All mushers will be subject to drug and alcohol testing under any of the following circumstances:

•   Whenever a race official reasonably suspects that the musher is under the influence of drugs or alcohol; or

•   On a random or chance basis, either individually or as a group.

For purposes of this policy, drugs are defined as marijuana, hashish, cocaine, opiates, amphetamines, phencyclidine or any other narcotic or controlled substance as defined by federal or state law.

To the extent practical, drug and alcohol testing will be conducted pursuant to the U.S. Department of Transportation Drug and Alcohol Testing Procedures (49 CFR Part 40, as amended) and Alaska Stat. 23.10.600-23.10.699, both of which are incorporated herein by reference. A musher will be deemed to be impaired if a detectable concentration of a drug, or the metabolites of such drug, is found in his or her system using the limits of detection established by a drug testing service or alcohol is found in his or her system at .04% BAC. Copies of the U.S. Department of Transportation Drug and Alcohol Testing Procedures and Alaska Stat. 23.10.600-23.10.699 are available for inspecting upon request.

A musher who tests positive for drug use or alcohol impairment is subject to immediate withdrawal from the Race. A refusal to participate in drug or alcohol testing will result in immediate withdrawal from the Race. Adulteration of a test specimen will be treated as a refusal to participate in drug or alcohol testing. Nothing in this policy is intended to require drug testing before a musher is sanctioned for suspected drug use or alcohol impairment that is supported by other evidence.

Rule 30 – Outside Assistance: No planned help is allowed throughout the Race. All care and feeding of dogs will be done only by that teams' musher. All dog maintenance and care of dog teams and gear in checkpoints will be done in the designated localized holding area. A musher relinquishing the care of his/her team to leave the checkpoint and or village without approval of the race marshal must withdraw from the Race. Common resources available to all mushers will not be considered outside assistance.

Rule 31 – No Man's Land: No man's land is the trail between Fort Davis Roadhouse and the official finish line in Nome. A musher need not relinquish the trail on demand in this area.

Rule 32 – One Musher per Team: Only one musher will be permitted per team and that musher must complete the entire race.

Rule 33 – Killing of Game Animals: In the event that an edible big game animal, i.e., moose, caribou, buffalo, is killed in defense of life or property, the musher must gut the animal and report the incident to a race official at the next checkpoint. Following teams must help gut the animal when possible. No teams may pass until the animal has been gutted and the musher killing the animal has proceeded. Any other animal killed in defense of life or property must be reported to a race official, but need not be gutted.

Rule 34 – Two-Way Communication Device, ELT or Satellite Tracking Device: No two-way communication device shall be allowed unless provided by ITC. Use of any electronic communication or tracking device shall not be permitted unless provided by the ITC.

Rule 35 – Navigation: Mushers are restricted to the use of traditional forms of navigation. This includes time, distance as known or measured on a map, speed as is computed with simple arithmetic and direction as indicated by magnetic compass. Electronic or mechanical devices that measure speed and direction are prohibited, i.e. Loran, night vision goggles and GPS'.

Rule 36 – Competitiveness: The race marshal shall have the authority to withdraw a team that is out of the competition and is no longer making a valid effort to compete. The race marshal also has the authority to withdraw a musher whose conduct, in the race marshal's sole and exclusive judgment, constitutes an unreasonable risk of harm to himself/herself, dogs or other persons.

VETERINARY ISSUES AND DOG CARE RULES

Rule 37 – Dog Care:

•   Dogs must be maintained in good condition. All water and food must be ingested voluntarily.

•   Dogs may not be brought into shelters except for race veterinarians' medical examination or
treatment. Dogs must be returned outside as soon as such examination or treatment is completed unless the dog is dropped from the race.

•   There will be no cruel or inhumane treatment of dogs. Cruel or inhumane treatment involves any action or inaction, which causes preventable pain or suffering to a dog.

Rule 38 – Harness and Cables: Dogs must leave checkpoints with functional, non-chafing harnesses. A musher must carry cable tie-out lines or have cable in the towline capable of securing the team. Equipment and team configurations deemed unsafe by race officials are prohibited.

Rule 39 – Drug Use: No oral or topical drug which may suppress the signs of illness or injury may be used on a dog. No injectables may be used in dogs participating in the Race. No other drugs or other artificial means may be used to drive a dog or cause a dog to perform or attempt to perform beyond its natural ability. The following drugs and procedures are prohibited:

- Anabolic Steroids
- Analgesics (prescriptive and non-prescriptive)
- Anesthetics
- Antihistamines
- Anti-inflammatory drugs including but not limited to:
- Cortico-steroids (the exception is for use on feet)
- Antiprostaglandins.
- Non-steroidals.
- Salicylates.
- DMSO.
- Bronchodilators
- Central Nervous System Stimulants
- Cough Suppressants
- Diuretics
- Muscle Relaxants
- Tranquilizers & Opiates
- Blood doping

Mibolerone (Cheque Drops) is permitted only for use as an estrus suppressant in intact females that have not had an ovario-hysterectomy. Megesterol acetate (Ovaban) is permitted for use of estrus suppression and medical conditions for which progesterone therapy is appropriate, as approved by the chief veterinarian.

Race veterinarians may utilize any of the listed drugs or other prohibited drugs necessary to maintain a dog's health, however, such dogs will be withdrawn from the race.

Drug Testing:

- Dogs are subject to the collection of urine or blood samples, at the discretion of the testing veterinarian, at any point from the pre-race examination until six (6) hours after the team's finish. The musher or a designee will remain with the dogs. All results will be sealed and signed for before the tests are considered complete.

• A musher must assist the veterinarian in collecting samples whenever requested. If blood or urine testing of a dog reveals any of the prohibitive drugs in the dog, this rule has been violated regardless of when such drugs were administered to the dog. Blood, urine and other test results will be made available upon request.

Rule 40 – Pre-Race Veterinary Exam: Veterinary paperwork, including Pre-Race Exam forms (one for each dog with proof of vaccination), Dog Microchip Identification Sheet (maximum 20), Verification of Deworming Form and the Veterinarian Signature Form (the letter from the chief veterinarian addressing the veterinarian who performs the physical exams which must be signed along with each Pre-Race Exam Form), has to be delivered to ITC Headquarters by the deadline of 5:00 p.m. on Wednesday, February 28. Non-compliance will result in a fine of $100.

Mushers will get appointments for blood tests and ECGs (EKGs) on first come first served basis, beginning at 8:00 a.m. Friday, December 1, 2006. Appointments must be made by December 20, 2006. The chief veterinarian will have the authority to deny entry to any dog if, after consultation with a veterinary cardiologist or internist (when available), it is the professional opinion of the chief veterinarian that the dog has an abnormality which may predispose it to a significant risk of injury or death.

A musher must have the team physicals performed at the official pre-race veterinary examination or by an ITC-approved veterinarian, on or after February 16, 2006. The following conditions will prohibit a dog from participating: seizures (epilepsy), syncope (fainting) and/or pregnancy.

A musher is permitted to have a maximum of 24 dogs screened (microchips, EKGs and blood work) in preparation for Iditarod 2007. (All 24 dogs must be screened at the original appointment date. There will be no additional screening after that time.) From these, a musher may select a maximum of 20 dogs for listing on the Dog Microchip Identification Sheet, which must be submitted to ITC Headquarters by the previously stated deadline of 5:00 p.m. on Wednesday, February 28. To be listed on the Microchip Identification Sheet, dogs must have had pre-race screening by Iditarod personnel, including a documented microchip implant number, an ECG (EKG) recording and blood work. In addition, each must have had a pre-race physical exam to be eligible to race. The musher may select his/her dogs for the start from any dogs previously qualified. Dogs for the restart may be selected from any dogs previously qualified and not run in another team on Saturday.

The maximum number of dogs permitted at the start will be determined by the Race Marshal. A maximum of 16 dogs may be selected for the restart. Once a dog has run in a team, that dog cannot be switched to another team.

All dogs entered in the race must have current distemper, hepatitis, parvo, and rabies vaccines. Proof of these vaccinations, except for rabies, must come from a veterinarian or a certified lay vaccinator or if administered by the musher, records must include type of vaccine, proof of purchase (i.e., receipt), and date of vaccination in writing. The distemper/hepatitis/parvo/vaccine must have been given between April 1, 2006, and February 18, 2007.

Proof of rabies vaccine must come from a licensed veterinarian or certified lay vaccinator. Rabies vaccines must be given no later than February 18, 2007 and must be current through April 1, 2007 according to Alaska State regulations.

All teams must be de-wormed for *Echinoccocus Multilocularis* with a medication approved by the ITC on or after February 21, 2007. The ITC is currently negotiating with the sponsor for donation of this de-worming medication. However, mushers should be prepared to pay for this medication if it is not available from the sponsor.

For those mushers who have volunteered and signed consent forms, ITC will be allowed to collect samples and gather data from dropped dogs and dogs that have completed the race, in the effort to gather information to improve dog care.

Rule 41 – Jurisdiction and Care: All dogs entered in the race are under the jurisdiction of the chief veterinarian and veterinary staff from the time they enter the staging area at the start until 72 hours after they have been released by the ITC veterinarians. The chief veterinarian shall have the authority to determine in his or her exclusive discretion whether any dogs require veterinary care and to select the provider, including treatment by medical specialists and or 24-hour care facilities, prior to an animal's release. In such case, financial responsibility shall be borne by the musher. In addition, the chief veterinarian will have immediate access to medical records and updated status reports of all dropped for up to 72 hours after their release. In the event that a death occurs within the 72-hour period following release, an ITC representative will participate in a necropsy of that animal.

Rule 42 – Expired Dog: All dog deaths are regrettable, but there are some that may be considered unpreventable.

Any dog that expires on the trail must be taken by the musher to a checkpoint. The musher may transport the dog to either the checkpoint just passed, or the upcoming checkpoint. An expired dog report must be completed by the musher and presented to a race official along with the dog.

All dog deaths will be treated as a priority, with every effort being made to determine the cause of death in a thorough and reliable manner.

•   The race marshal, or his/her appointed judges, will determine whether the musher should continue or be disqualified.

•   The chief veterinarian will cause a necropsy to be carried out by a board-certified pathologist at the earliest opportunity and shall make every attempt to determine the cause of death.

•   If a board-certified pathologist is not available to perform the necropsy within the time frame to preserve the tissues appropriately, (as determined by the race marshal), the gross necropsy and tissue collection will be performed by a trail veterinarian following the guidelines in the *Musher and Veterinary Handbook*.

•   These tissues will then be examined by a board-certified pathologist.

A musher will remain at the initial reporting checkpoint for up to, but no longer than, eight hours to commence the investigation. The musher and or his/her representative has the option to be present during the trail evaluation and necropsy.

This period is not to be used as a penalty. A musher will also make him/herself available at all future checkpoints to assist in the investigation. The race marshal, or his/her appointed judges, may release a musher before the eight hours have expired if the judge is satisfied that the musher is no longer needed to further the investigation. Dog deaths resulting in disqualification are:

- Signs of cruel, inhumane or abusive treatment
- Cause of death is heat stress, hyperthermia
- A musher will be disqualified if he/she had been advised in writing by a race veterinarian or judge to drop the dog at a previous checkpoint, but opted not to do so, unless the cause of death is clearly unrelated to this written recommendation.

The musher will not be penalized and may continue the race if:

- Cause of death can not be determined
- The cause of death is due to a circumstance, nature of trail, or force beyond the control of the musher. This recognizes the inherent risks of wilderness travel.
- Cause of death is from some unpreventable or previously undiagnosed medical condition.

It is the policy of the ITC to report a dog death to the public in a timely fashion. The ITC will accomplish this by:

- The race marshal shall immediately issue a press release to members of the media identifying the dog's death.
- Immediately following the gross necropsy, the race marshal will notify the musher of the results and will issue a press release containing the findings and the circumstances of the death.

Rule 43 – Dog Description: Only dogs suitable for arctic travel will be permitted to enter the race. Suitability will be determined by race officials.

Rule 44 – Dog Tags: The ITC will provide drivers with dog tags at the mushers' banquet. All dogs must wear tags and the tag numbers must correspond with the dog name and tag numbers written in the vet book. Only current tags are permitted.

Rule 45 – Dropped Dogs: All dogs that are dropped from the Race must be left at a designated checkpoint with a completed and signed dropped dog form. Any dropped dog must be left with four (4) pounds of dog food and a reliable chain or cable (16" to 18" in length) with a swivel snap and collar. Dropped dogs may be moved form the originating checkpoint to the closest dog collection area at Anchorage, McGrath, Unalakleet or Nome. Dogs may be shipped from the collection areas to a location designated by the musher at the musher's expense.

- Dogs dropped in ANCHORAGE, EAGLE RIVER & the restart are the musher's responsibility.
- GOLOVIN & NOME are not dog drops.
- Dogs dropped in ALL OTHER CHECKPOINTS will be transported by the ITC.

Dogs left unclaimed at Eagle River Correctional Center after four days after their arrival will incur boarding charges at the current rate, payable by the musher.

Rule 46 – Hauling Dogs: A musher may haul dogs in the sled at his/her discretion, however, the musher may not allow any of the dogs to be hauled by another team. Dogs must be hauled in a humane fashion and must be covered if conditions require.

FOOD DROPS AND LOGISTICS

Rule 47 – Shipping of Food and Gear: A musher must comply with shipping directions provided by the ITC. Each container must be clearly marked with name and destination and must weigh no more than 70 pounds. No boxes of any kind may be used as the primary container. No straw, charcoal, fuel or other combustible material, or hazardous materials (including lithium batteries) may be shipped through the ITC food drops. No cookers, plastic buckets, coolers or dog dishes may be shipped except with any sled that is shipped. Used items maybe removed from checkpoints with dropped sleds, by return mail or through the ITC.

Perishable food must be delivered to the ITC in a frozen state.

All mandatory food must be sent through Iditarod food drops. The ITC will provide and ship straw and fuel for the teams to the checkpoints. Additional food and gear may be shipped prior to the start but must be shipped to the checker. Gear or food drops damaged or lost may be replaced upon approval of the race marshal or designee.

Food-drop payment must be received by the ITC at time of delivery.

A musher's personal gear, equipment and supplies may not be transported along the trail by mechanized means without the consent of the race marshal.

Dog food left behind and dog food from scratched, withdrawn and disqualified mushers becomes the property of the ITC and may be used at the discretion of race officials.

Rule 48 – Shipping Amounts: An adequate amount of food is required to be shipped to the following checkpoints (minimum of 60 pounds combined weight of food and gear): Skwentna, Rainy Pass, Rohn, Nikolai, McGrath, Takotna, Ophir, Iditarod, Shageluk, Anvik, Grayling, Eagle Island, Kaltag, Unalakleet, Shaktoolik, Koyuk, Elim, White Mountain, Nome.

Food and/or gear will not be shipped to the checkpoints of Yentna, Finger Lake or Golovin.

The Safety checkpoint is optional for shipment of gear and/or food.

OFFICIALS, PENALTIES AND APPEALS

Rule 49 – Race Officials: The race marshal and judges are responsible for the enforcement of all ITC policies and race rules. Race officials shall consult with the chief veterinarian on all matters relating to dog care and treatment.

Rule 50 – Protests: A musher may protest any action of a competitor or race official that he/she feels is contrary to the intent of these rules. To be recognized as a legitimate protest, any action observed by a musher must be presented in writing at the next checkpoint and in no case more than twenty-four (24) hours after a musher finishes the race.

Rule 51– Penalties: Policy and rule infractions may result in issuance of warnings, monetary penalties, time penalties, censure, withdrawals or disqualification.

•   Warnings may be issued by any official for first time or minor violations.

•   Monetary penalties may be imposed up to $1,000 per violation. Such penalties may be deducted from prize money. A musher with unpaid fines may not enter future Iditarod races until such fines are paid.

•   Time penalties require a majority decision of a three-member panel of race officials appointed by the race marshal. Time penalties may be imposed up to a maximum of two (2) hours per infraction and will be added to the twenty-four (24) hour layover, the eight-hour layover on the Yukon River or the eight (8) hour layover at White Mountain. Time penalties will not be levied past White Mountain.

•   Withdrawal is a process that must be imposed by a three-judge panel, either by a majority or

unanimous vote, and which has the effect of involuntarily eliminating the musher and team from the race but which does not imply any deliberate misconduct or violation. The team and musher must leave the trail and will be assisted by the ITC.

•   Disqualifications require a unanimous decision of a three-member panel of race judges appointed by the race marshal. The chief veterinarian will be consulted in all cases involving cruel or inhumane treatment. Mushers shall be disqualified for rule infractions involving physical abuse of a dog, or for cheating or deliberate rule infractions that give a musher an unfair advantage over another musher. Mushers may also be disqualified for other acts involving cruel and inhumane treatment. It is intended that the nearest involved officials be included on the panel. The musher will be given the opportunity to present his case to each member of the panel prior to the decision. Disqualified and withdrawn teams must leave the trail or forfeit the right to enter future Iditarods.

•   Censure: The Board of Directors, following completion of the race, may censure a musher. A censure may include a warning, either public or private and may eliminate the musher from future races. A written warning, monetary penalty or disqualification must have occurred before censure.

Rule 52 – Appeals: Mushers may appeal race official decisions. Appeals pertaining to warnings or monetary fines must be presented in writing to the ITC within ten (10) days following the awards banquet. Appeals pertaining to censure must be presented in writing to the ITC within ten (10) days after receipt of the censure by the musher. Appeals pertaining to withdrawals, disqualifications or time penalties must be presented in writing to ITC within 10 days following the awards banquet. Appeals will be considered at an informal hearing before an appeals board appointed by the president of ITC, which will be held within forty-five (45) days of filing the appeal. Review by the appeals board is the exclusive, final and binding remedy for any dispute regarding application of the rules by race officials to a musher and that the decision of the appeals board is non-reviewable either in state or federal courts.

Appendix II

THE MUSHERS, 1973–2006

1973

1. Dick Wilmarth
2. Bobby Vent
3. Dan Seavey
4. George Attla
5. Herbert Nayokpuk
6. Isaac Okleasik
7. Dick Mackey
8. John Komak
9. John Coffin
10. Ron Aldrich
11. Bill Arpino
12. Bud Smyth
13. Ken Chase
14. Ron Oviak
15. Victor Kotongan
16. Robert
    and Owen Ivan
17. Rod Perry
18. Tom Mercer
19. Terry Miller
20. Howard Farley
21. Bruce Mitchell
22. John Schultz
SCRATCHED:
Hal Bartko
John Schultheis
Darrel Reynolds
Barry McAlpine
Slim Randles
Raymie Redington
John Luster
Alex Tatum
C. Killigrock
David Olson
Herbert Foster
Ford Reeves
    and Mike Schrieber
Casey Celusnik

1974

1. Carl Huntington
2. Warner Vent
3. Herbie Nayokpuk
4. Rudy Demoski
5. Dan Seavey
6. Ken Chase
7. Raymie Redington
8. Ron Aldrich
9. Joee Redington, Jr.
10. Dick Mackey
11. Joe Redington, Sr.
12. Tom Mercer
13. Jamie "Bud" Smith
14. Rod Perry
15. Dave Olson
16. Reuben Seetot
17. Robert Ivan
18. Victor Kotongan
19. Terry Adkins
20. Tim White
21. Desi Kamera
22. Clifton Jackson
23. Mary Shields
24. Lolly Medley
25. Joel Kottke
26. Red Olson
SCRATCHED:
Steve Murphy
Carl Topkok
Richard Korb
John Ace
Bernie Willis
Ward Olanna
John Luster
Don Rosevear
John Coffin
Wilbur Sampson
George Attla

Jack Schultheis
Ralph "Babe"
    Anderson
Jerry Riley
Bill Vaudrin
Warren Coffin
Tom Johnson
Isaac Okleasik

1975

1. Emmitt Peters
2. Jerry Riley
3. Joee Redington, Jr.
4. Herbert Nayokpuk
5. Joe Redington, Sr.
6. Henry Beatus
7. Dick Mackey
8. Ken Chase
9. Rudy Demoski
10. Eep Anderson
11. Allan Perry
12. Ray Jackson
13. Rick Mackey
14. Victor Kotongan
15. Ralph Lee
16. Robert Schlentner
17. Bill Cotter
18. Chris Camping
19. Bill Vaudrin
20. Darrell Reynolds
21. Richard Burnham
22. Jim Kershner
23. John Ace
24. Mike Sherman
25. Steve Fee
SCRATCHED:
Norman Vaughan
Edward Bosco

Hans Algottsen
Sandy Hamilton
Michael T. Holland
Ginger Burcham
Bobby Vent
Guy Blankenship
Terry McMullin
Lavon Barve
Carl Huntington
Walt Palmer
Charlie Fitka
Doug Bartko
Franklin Paniptchuk
John Komak

1976

1. Jerry Riley
2. Warner Vent
3. Harry Sutherland
4. Jamie "Bud" Smyth
5. Emmitt Peters
6. Ralph Mann
7. William Nelson
8. Dick Mackey
9. Tom Mercer
10. Rick Swenson
11. Joe May
12. Don Honea
13. Allan Perry
14. Ray Jackson
15. Ken Chase
16. Billy Demoski
17. Terry Adkins
18. Rudy Demoski
19. Jack Hooker
20. Ford Reeves
21. Babe Anderson
22. Lavon Barve
23. Jerry Austin
24. Ron Aldrich
25. Richard Burnham
26. Charlie Fitka

27. Steve Jones
28. Clarence Towarak
29. Alex Sheldon
30. William Solomon
31. Allan Marple
32. Peter Nelson
33. Jon Van Zyle
34. Dennis Corrington
SCRATCHED:
Joe Redington, Sr.
Norman Vaughan
Richard Hanks
Trent Long
Bob Schlentner
Peter Kakaruk
John Giannone
Lee Chamberlain
Oran Knox
Mel Fudge
Bruce Mitchell
Phillip Foxie
Steve Fee

1977

1. Rick Swenson
2. Jerry Riley
3. Warner Vent
4. Emmitt Peters
5. Joe Redington, Sr.
6. Dick Mackey
7. Don Honea
8. Robert Schlentner
9. Babe Anderson
10. Jack Hooker
11. Ken Chase
12. Alex Sheldon
13. Pete MacManus
14. Terry Adkins
15. Al Crane
16. Howard Albert
17. William Nelson
18. Roger Nordlum
19. Rod Perry

20. Richard Burnham
21. Stein Havard Fjestad
22. Bill Cotter
23. Rick Mackey
24. Sandy Hamilton
25. Bob Chlupach
26. Charlie Harrington
27. Eep Anderson
28. Jim Smarz
29. Duane Halverson
30. Peter Kakaruk
31. Randy DeKuiper
32. Dale Swartzentruber
33. Jerry Mercer
34. Varona Thompson
35. Jim Tofflemeire
36. Vasily Zamitkyn
SCRATCHED:
Don Montgomery
Tom Mathias
Ray Jackson
Rudy Demoski
Rick McConnell
Bob Watson
Ron Gould
Franklin Paniptchuk
John Ace
Dinah Knight
Jerry Austin
John Hancock
William Solomon

1978

1. Dick Mackey
2. Rick Swenson
3. Emmitt Peters
4. Ken Chase
5. Joe Redington, Sr.
6. Eep Anderson
7. Howard Albert
8. Robert Schlentner
9. Jerry Austin
10. Allan Perry

11. Sonny Lindner
12. Ron Aldrich
13. Pete MacManus
14. Bob Chlupach
15. Ron Tucker
16. Terry Adkins
17. Harry Sutherland
18. Richard Burnham
19. Susan Butcher
20. Varona Thompson
21. Joe Garnie
22. Jerry Mercer
23. Charlie Fitka
24. Ernie Baumgartner
25. Jack Goodwin
26. Rick McConnell
27. William Solomon
28. James Brandon
29. Shelley Vandiver
30. John Wood
31. Ray Gordon
32. Gary Campen
33. Norman Vaughan
34. Andrew Foxie
SCRATCHED:
Roger Roberts
Duke Bertke
Mike Demarco
Bill Rose
Babe Anderson

1979

1. Rick Swenson
2. Emmitt Peters
3. Sonny Lindner
4. Jerry Riley
5. Joe May
6. Don Honea
7. Howard Albert
8. Rick Mackey
9. Susan Butcher
10. Joe Redington, Sr.

11. Gary Hokkanen
12. Terry Adkins
13. Dick Peterson
14. Ken Chase
15. Ernie Baumgartner
16. Melvin Adkins
17. Bob Chlupach
18. Victor Kotongan
19. Keith Jones
20. Patty Friend
21. Brian Blandford
22. John Wood
23. Ron Aldrich
24. Eep Anderson
25. Myron Angstman
26. Walter Kaso
27. Jim Rowe
28. Steve Voltersen
29. Rick McConnell
30. Rome Gilman
31. Bud Smyth
32. Bill Rose
33. Steve Adkins
34. Cliff Sisson
35. Ron Brinkner
36. Del Allison
37. John Barron
38. Karl Clauson
39. Jerry LaVoie
40. Gayle Nienhauser
41. Richard Burmeister
42. Jon Van Zyle
43. Jim Lanier
44. Ron Gould
45. Don Montgomery
46. Prentice Harris
47. Gene Leonard
SCRATCHED:
Mark Couch
Isaac Okleasik
Herbie Nayokpuk
Kelly Wages

Terry McMullin
Lee Gardino
Clarence Towarak
Joe Garnie

1980

1. Joe May
2. Herbie Nayokpuk
3. Ernie Baumgartner
4. Rick Swenson
5. Susan Butcher
6. Roger Nordlum
7. Jerry Austin
8. Walter Kaso
9. Emmitt Peters
10. Donna Gentry
11. Marc Boily
12. Joe Garnie
13. Larry Smith
14. Bruce Johnson
15. Rudy Demoski
16. Dave Olson
17. Terry Adkins
18. Libby Riddles
19. Harold Ahmasuk
20. Henry Johnson
21. William Bartlett
22. Martin Buser
23. Jack Goodwin
24. DeeDee Jonrowe
25. Ken Chase
26. Bruce Denton
27. Clarence Shockley
28. John Cooper
29. Michael Harrington
30. Marjorie Ann Moore
31. Eric Poole
32. Douglas Sherrer
33. Ron Cortte
34. John Gartiez
35. Norman Vaughan
36. Barbara Moore

SCRATCHED:
Bill Boyko
Jan Masek
Ed Craver
Eugene R. Ivey
Larry Cogdill
Robert E. Neidig
John Eckles
Steven R. Conatser
Duke Bertke
Varona Thompson
Fred Jackson
John Barron
Dick Peterson
Lee Gardino
Don Honea, Sr.
Babe Anderson
Don Eckles
Frank Sampson
Sonny Lindner
Joe Redington, Sr.
Dick Mackey
Alton Walluk
Bruce Woods
Jerry Riley

1981

1. Rick Swenson
2. Sonny Lindner
3. Roger Nordlum
4. Larry Smith
5. Susan Butcher
6. Eep Anderson
7. Herbie Nayokpuk
8. Clarence Towarak
9. Rick Mackey
10. Terry Adkins
11. Duane Halverson
12. Emmitt Peters
13. Jerry Austin
14. Joe Redington, Sr.
15. Harry Sutherland

16. Joe Garnie
17. Gary Attla
18. Donna Gentry
19. Martin Buser
20. Libby Riddles
21. David Monson
22. Bruce Denton
23. John Barron
24. Gene Leonard
25. Bob Martin
26. Neil Eklund
27. Mark Freshwaters
28. Jeff King
29. Steve Flodin
30. Gary Whittemore
31. DeeDee Jonrowe
32. Sue Firmin
33. Mike Storto
34. Dan Zobrist
35. Dennis Boyer
36. Jan Masek
37. Burt Bomhoff
38. Jim Strong
SCRATCHED:
Frank Sampson
Harold Ahmasuk
William Webb
Ernie Baumgartner
Gordon Castanza
Douglas Sherrer
Bud Smyth
Ted English
Wes McIntyre
Willie French
Clifton Jackson
Bill Thompson
Jerry Riley
Myron Angstman
Ken Chase

1982

1. Rick Swenson

2. Susan Butcher
3. Jerry Austin
4. Emmitt Peters
5. Dave Monson
6. Ernie Baumgartner
7. Bob Chlupach
8. Don Honea, Sr.
9. Stan Zuray
10. Bruce Denton
11. Rick Mackey
12. Herbie Nayokpuk
13. Dean Osmar
14. Terry Adkins
15. Joe May
16. Marc Boily
17. Joe Redington, Sr.
18. Ed Foran
19. Guy Blankenship
20. John Stam
21. Alex Sheldon
22. Mitch Seavey
23. Glen Findlay
24. John Wood
25. Babe Anderson
26. Jim Strong
27. Ron Cortte
28. Larry Smith
29. Dean Painter
30. Ken Chase
31. Steve Gaber
32. Rose Albert
33. Jan Masek
34. Chris Deverill
35. Leroy Shank
36. Steve Flodin
37. Frank I. Brown
38. Mark Rosser
39. Bill Yankee
40. James Cole
41. Richard Burmeister
42. Rick Tarpey
43. Erick Buetow
44. Rome Gilman

45. Jack Studer
46. Ralph Bradley
SCRATCHED:
John Barron
Michael Harrington
Steve Haver
Sue Firmin
Smokey Moff
Bill Rose
Norman Vaughan
Gary Whittemore

1983

1. Rick Mackey
2. Eep Anderson
3. Larry Smith
4. Herbie Nayokpuk
5. Rick Swenson
6. Lavon Barve
7. Duane Halverson
8. Sonny Lindner
9. Susan Butcher
10. Roger Legaard
11. Joe Runyan
12. Guy Blankenship
13. Dave Monson
14. Sue Firmin
15. DeeDee Jonrowe
16. Howard Albert
17. Bruce Denton
18. Dave Olson
19. Emmitt Peters
20. John Barron
21. Neil Eklund
22. Burt Bomhoff
23. Roxy Woods
24. Walter Kaso
25. Eric Buetow
26. Jim Strong
27. Ken Hamm
28. Vern Halter

29. Shannon Poole
30. William Hayes
31. Walter Williams
32. Christine O'Gar
33. Ted English
34. Bud Smyth
35. Ron Brennan
36. Wes McIntyre
37. Ken Johnson
38. Steve Rieger
39. Connie Frerichs
40. Ray Dronenburg
41. Gary Paulsen
42. Ed Forstner
43. Mark Nordman
44. Dick Barnum
45. David Wolfe
46. Leroy Shank
47. Robert Gould
48. Fritz Kirsch
49. Steve Haver
50. Ron Gould
51. Pam Flowers
52. Norman Vaughan
53. Norm MacAlpine
54. Scott Cameron
SCRATCHED:
Terry Adkins
Eugene R. Ivey
Gene Leonard
Beverly Jerue
William Cowart
Alex Sheldon
Bob Bright
Saul Paniptchuk
Ken Chase
Clifton Cadzow
DISQUALIFIED:
Les Atherton
Hal Bartko
Doug Bartko
Jan Masek

1984

1. Dean Osmar
2. Susan Butcher
3. Joe Garnie
4. Marc Boily
5. Jerry Austin
6. Rick Swenson
7. Joe Redington, Sr.
8. Terry Adkins
9. John Cooper
10. Larry Smith
11. Vern Halter
12. Burt Bomhoff
13. Rusty Miller
14. Mark Freshwaters
15. Bob Chlupach
16. Ed Foran
17. Emmitt Peters
18. Rick Armstrong
19. Ray Gordon
20. John Barron
21. Jim Strong
22. Bob Toll
23. Eep Anderson
24. Gordon Castanza
25. Ron Cortte
26. Jerry Raychel
27. Diana Dronenburg
28. Sue Firmin
29. Rick Mackey
30. DeeDee Jonrowe
31. Dave Olson
32. Gary Whittemore
33. Eric Buetow
34. Frank Bettine
35. Kari Skogen
36. Calvin Lauwers
37. Dan Cowan
38. Francine Bennis
39. Rick Atkinson
40. Jim Lanier

41. David Scheer
42. Steve Peek
43. Fred Agree
44. Ed Borden
45. Bill Mackey
SCRATCHED:
Ted English
James Cole
Jan Masek
Dave Aisenbrey
Gene Leonard
Ray Dronenburg
Gordon Brinker
Connie Frerichs
Don Honea, Sr.
Lolly Medley
Larry Cogdill
Brian Johnson
Armen Khatchikian
Miki Collins
Steve Gaber
William Thompson
Mel Adkins
Bob Sunder
Darrel Reynolds
Vern Cherneski
Ron Brennan
DISQUALIFIED:
Guy Blankenship

1985

1. Libby Riddles
2. Duane Halverson
3. John Cooper
4. Rick Swenson
5. Rick Mackey
6. Vern Halter
7. Guy Blankenship
8. Herbert Nayokpuk
9. Sonny Lindner
10. Lavon Barve
11. Tim Moerlein

12. Emmitt Peters
13. Tim Osmar
14. Jerry Austin
15. Terry Adkins
16. Roger Nordlum
17. Glen Findlay
18. John Barron
19. Raymie Redington
20. Burt Bomhoff
21. Jacques Philip
22. Bob Bright
23. Peter Fromm
24. Steve Flodin
25. Warner Vent
26. Ron Robbins
27. Kazuo Kojima
28. Nathan Underwood
29. Betsy McGuire
30. Kevin Saiki
31. Earl Norris
32. Kevin Fulton
33. John Coble
34. Allan Cheshire
35. Victor Jorge
36. Fred Agree
37. Claire Philip
38. John Ace
39. Rick Armstrong
40. Monique Bene
SCRATCHED:
David Aisenbrey
Terry Hinesly
Susan Butcher
Ted English
Jan Masek
Joe Redington, Sr.
Fred Jackson
Victor Kotongan
Gary Paulsen
Ray Dronenburg
Joseph Maillelle, Sr.
Terry McMullin
Dennis Towarak

Ernie Baumgartner
Rudy Demoski
Norman Vaughan
Armen Khatchikian
Scott Cameron
Chuck Schaeffer
DISQUALIFIED:
Bobby Lee
Wes McIntyre

1986

1. Susan Butcher
2. Joe Garnie
3. Rick Swenson
4. Joe Runyan
5. Duane Halverson
6. John Cooper
7. Lavon Barve
8. Jerry Austin
9. Terry Adkins
10. Rune Hesthammer
11. John Barron
12. Guy Blankenship
13. Tim Moerlein
14. Bob Chlupach
15. Jerry Riley
16. Vern Halter
17. Gary Whittemore
18. Ted English
19. Nina Hotvedt
20. Rick Atkinson
21. Rusty Miller
22. Peter Sapin
23. Frank Torres
24. Paul Johnson
25. Martin Buser
26. John Wood
27. Dan MacEachen
28. Jerry Raychel
29. Raymie Redington
30. Mike Pemberton
31. David Olesen

32. Steve Bush
33. Kari Skogen
34. Gordon Brinker
35. Bobby Lee
36. Ron Robbins
37. Dave Scheer
38. Gordon Hubbard
39. Matt Desalernos
40. Allan Cheshire
41. Ray Lang
42. Roger Roberts
43. Allen Miller
44. Armen Khatchikian
45. Don McQuown
46. Mike Lawless
47. Mark Jackson
48. Joe LeFaive
49. Peter Thomann
50. Pat Danly
51. Bill Hall
52. Bill Davidson
53. Scott Cameron
54. Stan Ferguson
55. Mike Peterson
SCRATCHED:
Abel Akpik
John Anderson
Frank Bettine
Roger Bliss
Ron Brennan
Joe Carpenter
Jim Darling
William Cowart
Ray Dronenburg
Don Honea
Fred Jackson
Rick Mackey
Jan Masek
Earl Norris
Joe Redington, Sr.
Douglas Sheldon
John Stam
Norman Vaughan

1987

1. Susan Butcher
2. Rick Swenson
3. Duane Halverson
4. Tim Osmar
5. Jerry Austin
6. Joe Runyan
7. Lavon Barve
8. Ted English
9. John Cooper
10. Martin Buser
11. Joe Garnie
12. Guy Blankenship
13. Jerry Riley
14. Diana Dronenburg
15. Stephen Adkins
16. Matt Desalernos
17. Harry Sutherland
18. Robin Jacobson
19. Bruce Johnson
20. Jacques Philip
21. Sue Firmin
22. DeeDee Jonrowe
23. Terry Adkins
24. Gary Whittemore
25. Herbie Nayokpuk
26. Claire Philip
27. Gary Guy
28. David J. Olesen
29. Don McEwen
30. Kazuo Kojima
31. Bruce Barton
32. Dick Mackey
33. Joe Redington, Sr.
34. Dennis J. Lozano
35. Nels Anderson
36. John Coble
37. Michael V. Owens
38. Roger Roberts
39. Pat Danly
40. Bill Chisholm
41. Henry Horner

42. Caleb Slemons
43. Mike Lawless
44. Roy Wade
45. John T. Gourley
46. Don McQuown
47. Matt Ace
48. Brian Johnson
49. Andre Monnier
50. Rhoda Karella
SCRATCHED:
Peter Thomann
Rick Mackey
Raymie Redington
John Barron
Burt Bomhoff
Gordon Hubbard
Libby Riddles
Gordon Brinker
Joe LeFaive
David Aisenbrey
WITHDRAWN:
Carolyn Muegge
Tony Burch
Norman Vaughan

1988

1. Susan Butcher
2. Rick Swenson
3. Martin Buser
4. Joe Garnie
5. Joe Redington, Sr.
6. Herbie Nayokpuk
7. Rick Mackey
8. Lavon Barve
9. DeeDee Jonrowe
10. Robin Jacobson
11. Jerry Austin
12. Jan Masek
13. Lucy Nordlum
14. Jacques Philip
15. Bill Cotter
16. Tim Osmar

17. Dan MacEachen
18. John Patten
19. Harry Sutherland
20. Matt Desalernos
21. Bill Hall
22. Darwin McLeod
23. Horst Maas
24. Ted English
25. Jerry Raychel
26. John Barron
27. Dewey Halverson
28. Peter Thomann
29. Conrad Saussele
30. Burt Bomhoff
31. Frank Teasley
32. Peryll Kyzer
33. Ken Chase
34. Babe Anderson
35. Ian MacKenzie
36. Mike Tvenge
37. Mark Merrill
38. John Suter
39. John Gourley
40. Jennifer Gourley
41. Peter Kelly
42. Tim Mowry
43. Matt Ace
44. Gordon Brinker
45. Lesley Anne Monk
SCRATCHED:
Tim Moerlein
Terry Adkins
Joe Runyan
Brian Carver
Ray Dronenburg
Norman Vaughan
DISQUALIFIED:
Stan Ferguson

1989

1. Joe Runyan
2. Susan Butcher
3. Rick Swenson

4. DeeDee Jonrowe
5. Lavon Barve
6. Martin Buser
7. Guy Blankenship
8. Rick Mackey
9. Joe Redington, Sr.
10. Tim Osmar
11. Jacques Philip
12. Matt Desalernos
13. Bob Chlupach
14. John Barron
15. Joe Garnie
16. Libby Riddles
17. Jerry Riley
18. Bill Cotter
19. Frank Teasley
20. Terry Adkins
21. Richard Self
22. Jerry Austin
23. Mitch Brazin
24. Diana Dronenburg
25. Jamie Nelson
26. Linwood Fiedler
27. Tim Mowry
28. Bill Cavaney
29. Karin Schmidt
30. Bernie Willis
31. Pat Danly
32. Kathy Halverson
33. Kazuo Kojima
34. Frank Winkler
35. Conner Thomas
36. John Suter
37. Duane Lamberts
38. Bob Hoyte
SCRATCHED:
Kevin Saiki
Carolyn Vaughan
Joe LeFaive
Michael Madden
Bill Chisolm
Gary Whittemore
Mike Ross

David Aisenbrey
Norman Vaughan
Roger Roberts
Jan Masek

1990

1. Susan Butcher
2. Joe Runyan
3. Lavon Barve
4. Tim Osmar
5. DeeDee Jonrowe
6. Robin Jacobson
7. Rick Swenson
8. Linwood Fiedler
9. Joe Garnie
10. Martin Buser
11. Bill Cotter
12. Rick Mackey
13. Michael Madden
14. Jacques Philip
15. Sonny Russell
16. John Barron
17. Matt Desalernos
18. John Gourley
19. Jerry Austin
20. Bill Chisholm
21. Dan MacEachen
22. Norm Stoppenbrink
23. Mike Owens
24. Terry Adkins
25. Joe Redington, Sr.
26. Mitch Brazin
27. Kevin Saiki
28. Diana Dronenburg
29. Bob Chlupach
30. Harry Sutherland
31. Don McEwen
32. Raymie Redington
33. Frank Winkler
34. Bill Hall
35. Beverly Masek
36. Malcolm Vance

37. Roy Wade
38. Roy Monk
39. Dave Breuer
40. Duane Lamberts
41. Emmitt Peters
42. Bob Hickel
43. Macgill Adams
44. Lynda Plettner
45. John Suter
46. Larry Harris
47. Greg Tibbetts
48. Bryan Moline
49. Jim Wood
50. Bert Hanson
51. Peter Kelly
52. Pecos Humphreys
53. Bill Davidson
54. Lorren Weaver
55. Lars Ekstrand
56. Larry Munoz
57. John Ace
58. Paul Byrd
59. Terry Hinesly
60. Norman Vaughan
61. Steve Haver
SCRATCHED:
Guy Blankenship
Tim Mundy
Chuck Schaeffer
Pascal Nicoud
Mike Ross
Frank Teasley
Leslie Monk
Joe LeFaive
DISQUALIFIED:
Jerry Riley

1991

1. Rick Swenson
2. Martin Buser
3. Susan Butcher
4. Tim Osmar
5. Joe Runyan

6. Frank Teasley
7. DeeDee Jonrowe
8. Matt Desalernos
9. Rick Mackey
10. Bill Cotter
11. Kate Persons
12. Jeff King
13. Jacques Philip
14. Jerry Austin
15. Michael Madden
16. Ketil Reitan
17. Lavon Barve
18. Peryll Kyzer
19. Terry Adkins
20. Bill Jack
21. Beverly Masek
22. Laird Barron
23. Joe Garnie
24. Rick Armstrong
25. Linwood Fiedler
26. Burt Bomhoff
27. Dan MacEachen
28. Dave Olesen
29. Raymie Redington
30. Dave Allen
31. Joe Redington, Sr.
32. Jerry Raychel
33. Mark Nordman
34. Malcolm Vance
35. Macgill Adams
36. Nikolai Ettyne
37. Alexander Reznyuk
38. Tony Shoogukwruk
39. Rollin Westrum
40. Brian Stafford
41. John Suter
42. Roger Roberts
43. Larry Munoz
44. Jim Cantor
45. Terry Seaman
46. Kazuo Kojima
47. Rich Bosela
48. Pat Danly

49. Dave Breuer
50. Chris Converse
51. Sepp Herrman
52. Lynda Plettner
53. Jon Terhune
54. Gunner Johnson
55. Urtha Lenharr
56. Tom Daily
57. Mark Williams
58. Catherine Mormile
59. Don Mormile
60. Brian O'Donoghue
SCRATCHED:
David Aisenbrey
Nels Anderson
Roy Monk
Gary Moore
John Ace
Sonny Russell
Robin Jacobson
Steve Fossett
Alan Garth
Bill Peele
Bobby Lee
Barry Lee
Ken Chase
John Barron
Gary Whittemore
DISQUALIFIED:
Joe Carpenter

1992

1. Martin Buser
2. Susan Butcher
3. Tim Osmar
4. Rick Swenson
5. DeeDee Jonrowe
6. Jeff King
7. Vern Halter
8. Rick Mackey
9. Doug Swingley
10. Ketil Reitan
11. Matt Desalernos

12. Bruce Lee
13. Claire Philip
14. Ed Iten
15. Bill Cotter
16. Kate Persons
17. Lavon Barve
18. John Barron
19. Dan MacEachen
20. Joe Garnie
21. Kathy Swenson
22. Sonny Lindner
23. Beverly Masek
24. Jerry Austin
25. Linwood Fiedler
26. Dave Olesen
27. Bill Jack
28. Frank Teasley
29. Rick Armstrong
30. Terry Adkins
31. Bob Chlupach
32. Burt Bomhoff
33. Bill Hall
34. Gary Whittemore
35. Tomas Israelsson
36. Kathy Tucker
37. Susan Cantor
38. Roy Monk
39. Lynda Plettner
40. Norm Stoppenbrink
41. Joe Redington, Sr.
42. Raymie Redington
43. Charlie Boulding
44. Mike Williams
45. Nels Anderson
46. Kim Teasley
47. Steve Fossett
48. Jon Terhune
49. Bob Holder
50. Jim Oehlschlaeger
51. Cliff Roberson
52. Pete Johnson
53. Steve Christon
54. Skin Wysocki

55. Mellen Shea
56. Bill Bass
57. Bob Hickel
58. Debbie Corral
59. James Reiter
60. Lorren Weaver
61. Jim Davis
62. John Peterson
63. Vern Cherneski
SCRATCHED:
Tim Mundy
Catherine Mormile
Carolyn Vaughan
Norman Vaughan
William Orazietti
Robin Jacobson
Pascal Nicoud
Emmitt Peters
Sonny Russell
Joe Runyan
Eep Anderson
Krista Maciolek
Bob Ernissee

1993

1. Jeff King
2. DeeDee Jonrowe
3. Rick Mackey
4. Susan Butcher
5. Tim Osmar
6. Martin Buser
7. Matt Desalernos
8. Doug Swingley
9. Rick Swenson
10. Bruce Lee
11. Vern Halter
12. Joe Runyan
13. Claire Philip
14. Kathy Swenson
15. John Barron
16. Joe Garnie
17. Linwood Fiedler

18. Sonny Lindner
19. Bill Cotter
20. Kate Persons
21. Dan MacEachen
22. David Olesen
23. Jerry Austin
24. Laird Barron
25. Kathy Tucker
26. Diana Dronenburg
27. Frank Teasley
28. Lynda Plettner
29. Terry Adkins
30. Dewey Halverson
31. Mike Williams
32. Mark Nordman
33. Bob Holder
34. Jason Barron
35. Keizo Funatsu
36. Ketil Reitan
37. Pecos Humphreys
38. Peryll Kyzer
39. Jim Oehlschlaeger
40. Skin Wysocki
41. Jerry Louden
42. Pat Danly
43. Stan Smith
44. Jack Goode
45. Roger Haertel
46. Paul Rupple
47. Joe Carpenter
48. Mark Chapoton
49. Kirsten Bey
50. Bert Hanson
51. Harry Caldwell
52. John Peterson
53. Spencer Thew
54. Lloyd Gilbertson
FINISHER:
Beverly Masek
SCRATCHED:
Julius Burgert
Norman Lee
Terry Hinesly

Val Aron
Gary Whittemore
David Aisenbrey
Gary Moore
Robin Jacobson
Rick Townsend
Robert Morgan
Lavon Barve
John Shandelmeier
DISQUALIFIED:
Dave Branholm

1994

1. Martin Buser
2. Rick Mackey
3. Jeff King
4. Rick Swenson
5. Bill Cotter
6. Doug Swingley
7. Charlie Boulding
8. Tim Osmar
9. DeeDee Jonrowe
10. Susan Butcher
11. Matt Desalernos
12. Kate Persons
13. Vern Halter
14. Peryll Kyzer
15. Robin Jacobson
16. David Olesen
17. Ramy Brooks
18. Linwood Fiedler
19. Diana Dronenburg
20. Kenth Fjelborg
21. Ramey Smyth
22. Jerry Austin
23. Ketil Reitan
24. Bruce Lee
25. Laird Barron
26. Frank Teasley
27. Stan Smith
28. Mike Williams
29. Lynda Plettner

30. Bill Hall
31. Bob Holder
32. Gus Guenther
33. Terry Adkins
34. Jack Berry
35. Krista Maciolek
36. Robert Somers
37. Aaron Burmeister
38. Cliff Roberson
39. Simon Kinneen
40. Bob Morgan
41. Steve Adkins
42. Dave Branholm
43. Bob Ernissee
44. Harry P. Caldwell
45. Ron Aldrich
46. Jon Terhune
47. Kazuo Kojima
48. Roger Bliss
49. Bruce Moroney
50. Mark Chapoton
SCRATCHED:
Beth Baker
Lisa M. Moore
Lloyd Gilbertson
Mark Nordman
Jamie Nelson
Chris Converse
Rick Townsend
Catherine Mormile

1995

1. Doug Swingley
2. Martin Buser
3. Bill Cotter
4. DeeDee Jonrowe
5. Charlie Boulding
6. Rick Mackey
7. Jeff King
8. Vern Halter
9. Tim Osmar
10. Rick Swenson
11. Peryll Kyzer

12. John Barron
13. Linwood Fiedler
14. Matt Desalernos
15. David Sawatzky
16. Ramy Brooks
17. Jerry Austin
18. David Olesen
19. Ramey Smith
20. Mitch Seavey
21. John Gourley
22. Mark Wildermuth
23. David Milne
24. Randy Adkins
25. Harry Caldwell
26. Jack Berry
27. Art Church
28. Cliff Roberson
29. Dave Branholm
30. Robert Salazar
31. Bob Holder
32. Kazuo Kojima
33. Libby Riddles
34. David Dalton
35. Don Lyrek
36. Nicolas Pattaroni
37. Pat Danly
38. Paula Gmerek
39. Rollin Westrum
40. Robert Bundtzen
41. Wayne Curtis
42. Jon Terhune
43. Nikolai Ettyne
44. Kjell Risung
45. Susan Whiton
46. Max Hall
47. Tim Triumph
48. Larry Williams
49. Ben Jacobson
SCRATCHED:
Andy Sterns
Kathleen Swenson
Diana Moroney
Robert Somers

Pecos Humphreys
Barrie Raper
Lorren Weaver
Don Bowers
Keizo Funatsu
Bob Bright

1996

1. Jeff King
2. Doug Swingley
3. Martin Buser
4. Tim Osmar
5. DeeDee Jonrowe
6. Bill Cotter
7. Charlie Boulding
8. David Sawatzky
9. Vern Halter
10. Peryll Kyzer
11. Ramy Brooks
12. David Scheer
13. Robin Jacobson
14. Lavon Barve
15. Mitch Seavey
16. John Barron
17. Linwood Fiedler
18. Cim Smyth
19. Roger Dahl
20. Sven Engholm
21. Jerry Austin
22. Johnny Baker
23. Tomas Israelsson
24. Dewey Halverson
25. Bruce Lee
26. Diana Moroney
27. Paul Gebhardt
28. Andy Willis
29. Dave Olesen
30. Nicolas Pattaroni
31. Conner Thomas
32. Steve Adkins
33. Kazuo Kojima

34. Michael Nosko
35. Harry Caldwell
36. Mike Weber
37. Jim Davis
38. Randy Romenesko
39. Susan Whiton
40. Lori Townsend
41. Bill Gallea
42. Mark Nordman
43. Aaron Burmeister
44. Rob Carss
45. Ararad Khatchikian
46. Dave Branholm
47. Lisa Moore
48. Don Bowers
49. Andy Sterns
SCRATCHED:
Bill Hall
Roy Monk
Rich Bosela
Stan Zuray
Jack Berry
Kjell Risung
Mark Black
WITHDRAWN:
Rick Swenson*
Ralph Ray
Linda Joy
Bob Bright
* Decision to withdraw Rick Swenson
was reversed by the Appeals Board.

1997

1. Martin Buser
2. Doug Swingley
3. Jeff King
4. DeeDee Jonrowe
5. Vern Halter
6. Lavon Barve
7. Bill Cotter
8. Ramy Brooks
9. Peryll Kyzer
10. Tim Osmar

11. John Baker
12. Sven Engholm
13. Charlie Boulding
14. Paul Gebhardt
15. Ramey Smyth
16. Mitch Seavey
17. Linwood Fiedler
18. Mike Williams
19. David Sawatzky
20. Kris Swanguarin
21. Nick Pattaroni
22. Michael Nosko
23. Jack Berry
24. Krista Maciolek
25. Raymie Redington
26. Harry Caldwell
27. Robert Bundtzen
28. Jean Lacroix
29. Randy Adkins
30. Keli Mahoney
31. Ross Adam
32. Mark Lindstrom
33. Al Hardman
34. Shawn Sidelinger
35. Dan Seavey
36. Joe Redington, Sr.
37. Wayne Curtis
38. Bill Bass
39. Bob Hickel
40. Don Bowers
41. Suzan Amundsen
42. Sonny King
43. Jerome Longo
44. Ken Chase
SCRATCHED:
John Barron
Dave Branholm
Ted English
Bob Ernissee
Max Hall
Linda Joy
Jerry Raychel

James Ritchie
Lori Townsend

1998

1. Jeff King
2. DeeDee Jonrowe
3. Charlie Boulding
4. Mitch Seavey
5. John Baker
6. Ramey Smyth
7. Martin Buser
8. Linwood Fiedler
9. Doug Swingley
10. Vern Halter
11. Rick Swenson
12. John Barron
13. Paul Gebhardt
14. Sven Engholm
15. David Sawatzky
16. Joe Garnie
17. Tim Osmar
18. Ramy Brooks
19. Bill Cotter
20. Mark May
21. Christopher Knott
22. Zack Steer
23. Mike Williams
24. Juan Alcina
25. Sonny King
26. Raymie Redington
27. Steve Adkins
28. Harry Caldwell
29. Hans Gatt
30. David Milne
31. Robin Jacobson
32. Ted English
33. Lynda Plettner
34. Shawn Sidelinger
35. Jerome Longo
36. Matt Hayashida
37. Andy Willis
38. Ross Adam

39. James Ritchie
40. Gus Guenther
41. Stephen Carrick
42. Jim Lanier
43. Jeremy Gebauer
44. Sam Maxwell
45. Kimarie Hanson
46. Linda Joy
47. Bill Snodgrass
48. Cindy Gallea
49. Chris Lund
50. Matthew Giblin
51. Brad Pozarnsky
SCRATCHED:
Terry Adkins
Suzan Amundsen
Jack Berry
Don Bowers
Rob Carss
Ken Chase
Marie Hayashida
Dave Lindquist
Keli Mahoney
Roy Monk
Michael Nosko
Kris Swanguarin

1999

1. Doug Swingley
2. Martin Buser
3. Vern Halter
4. Rick Swenson
5. Charlie Boulding
6. Paul Gebhardt
7. Jeff King
8. John Baker
9. Sven Engholm
10. Ed Iten
11. Mitch Seavey
12. Ramey Smyth
13. Linwood Fiedler
14. Bill Cotter

15. Dave Sawatzky
16. Rick Mackey
17. Joe Garnie
18. Tim Osmar
19. Harald Tunheim
20. Christopher Knott
21. Hans Gatt
22. Sonny King
23. Mike Williams
24. Sonny Lindner
25. Juan Alcina
26. Ken Anderson
27. Jerome Longo
28. Robert Bundtzen
29. Peryll Kyzer
30. Mike Nosko
31. Russell Lane
32. Raymie Redington
33. Matt Hayashida
34. Frank Teasley
35. Shawn Sidelinger
36. Jon Little
37. Max Hall
38. Lynda Plettner
39. Aaron Burmeister
40. Dario Daniels
41. Bill Hall
42. Jim Lanier
43. Jim Gallea
44. Don Bowers
45. Judy Currier
46. Jeremy Gebauer
SCRATCHED:
John Barron
Harry Caldwell
Steve Carrick
Steve Crouch
Dan Dent
Ted English
DeeDee Jonrowe
Linda Joy
Robert Moore

2000

1. Doug Swingley
2. Paul Gebhardt
3. Jeff King
4. Ramy Brooks
5. Charlie Boulding
6. Dick Mackey
7. Martin Buser
8. Rick Swenson
9. Mitch Seavey
10. Bill Cotter
11. Ramey Smyth
12. Hans Gatt
13. Bruce Lee
14. Zack Steer
15. John Barron
16. Tim Osmar
17. Juan Alcina
18. Sonny King
19. Linwood Fiedler
20. DeeDee Jonrowe
21. Vern Halter
22. John Baker
23. Jon Little
24. Ed Iten
25. Harald Tunheim
26. David Sawatzky
27. Tony Willis
28. Mike Williams
29. Raymie Redington
30. Aaron Burmeister
31. Diana Moroney
32. Joran Freeman
33. Bryan Imus
34. Nils Hahn
35. David Milne
36. Russell Lane
37. Al Hardman
38. James Ritchie
39. Mike Nosko
40. Emmitt Peters
41. Ross Adam

42. Jerome Longo
43. Shawn Sidelinger
44. Jamie Nelson
45. Billy Snodgrass
46. Blake Freking
47. Max Hall
48. John Dixon
49. Roy Monk
50. Steve Adkins
51. Aaron Peck
52. John Bramante
53. Anna Bondarenko
54. Paul Ellering
55. Kevin Korteum
56. Bob Hempstead
57. Caleb Banse
58. Vickie Talbot
59. Ed de la Billiere
60. Dan Govoni
61. Trisha Kolegar
62. Bill McKee
63. Dan Dent
64. Melanie Gould
65. James Wheeler
66. Lynda Plettner
67. Dave Tresino
68. Fedor Konyukhov

SCRATCHED:
Jerry Riley
Karen Ramstead
Rob Gregor
Bill Bass
Cindy Gallea
Shane Goosen
Mike Murphy
David Straub
Rich Bosela
Nelson Shugart
Harry Caldwell
Ted English

WITHDRAWN:
Neen Brown

2001

1. Doug Swingley
2. Linwood Fiedler
3. Jeff King
4. Rick Swenson
5. Paul Gebhardt
6. John Baker
7. Rick Mackey
8. Jerry Riley
9. Sonny King
10. DeeDee Jonrowe
11. Vern Halter
12. Ramy Brooks
13. Ramey Smith
14. Jessie Royer
15. Jon Little
16. Ed Iten
17. Andy Moderow
18. Tim Osmar
19. Hans Gatt
20. Charlie Boulding
21. Sonny Lindner
22. Nils Hahn
23. Juan Alcina
24. Martin Buser
25. Thomas Tetz
26. Bill Cotter
27. Russell Lane
28. Dan Govoni
29. Aaron Burmeister
30. Gwen Holdman
31. Robert Bundtzen
32. Jerome Longo
33. Aliy Zirkle
34. Raymie Redington
35. Ray Redington, Jr.
36. Lance Mackey
37. Mike Williams
38. Cindy Gallea
39. John Barron
40. Wally Robinson
41. Bob Chlupach

42. Mitch Seavey
43. Danny Seavey
44. Dan Seavey
45. Palmer Sagoonick
46. Morton Fonseca
47. Ron Koczaja
48. Bruce Moroney
49. Jim Lanier
50. Peryll Kyzer
51. Wayne Curtis
52. Beth Manning
53. Clinton Warnke
54. Buck Church
55. Roy Monk
56. Dave Tresino
57. Karen Ramstead
SCRATCHED:
Steve Carrick
Rob Carss
Art Church
Devon Currier
Pedro Curuchet
Chuck King
Mike Nosko
Ryan Redington
David Straub
WITHDRAWN:
Jason Halseth
Robert Morgan

2002

1. Martin Buser
2. Ramy Brooks
3. John Baker
4. Jon Little
5. Vern Halter
6. Jeff King
7. Ramey Smyth
8. Charlie Boulding
9. Robert Sørlie
10. Kjetil Backen
11. Mitch Seavey

12. Harald Tunheim
13. Sonny Lindner
14. Ray Redington, Jr.
15. Tim Osmar
16. DeeDee Jonrowe
17. Jerry Riley
18. Ken Anderson
19. Rick Swenson
20. Lynda Plettner
21. Al Hardman
22. John Barron
23. Hans Gatt
24. Bruce Lee
25. Jim Lanier
26. Peter Bartlett
27. Bill Cotter
28. Sonny King
29. Aliy Zirkle
30. Jim Gallea
31. Robert Bundtzen
32. Keith Aili
33. Stan Passananiti
34. Nils Hahn
35. Gerald Sousa
36. Palmer Sagoonick
37. Melanie Gould
38. Mike Williams
39. Garth Eldson
40. Doug Swingley
41. Harmony (Kanavale) Barron
42. Jason Barron
43. Daniel Vetch
44. Jim Oehlschlaeger
45. Nikolai Ettyne
46. Kelly Williams
47. Lisa Frederic
48. John Bramante
49. Karen Land
50. Devon Currier
51. Lesley Monk
52. G. B. Jones
53. Bill Borden

54. Ken Chase
55. David Straub
SCRATCHED:
Mark Black
Burt Bomhoff
Linwood Fiedler
Ellen Halverson
Rick Horstman
Lance Mackey
Sandy McKee
Judy Merritt
Perry Solmonson

2003

1. Robert Sørlie
2. Ramy Brooks
3. Jeff King
4. Martin Buser
5. Ken Anderson
6. Linwood Fiedler
7. Ramey Smyth
8. John Baker
9. Ed Iten
10. Sonny Lindner
11. Rick Swenson
12. Mitch Seavey
13. Jon Little
14. Aliy Zirkle
15. Ray Redington, Jr.
16. Aaron Burmeister
17. Bruce Lee
18. DeeDee Jonrowe
19. Jessica Hendricks
20. Jessie Royer
21. Vern Halter
22. Tim Osmar
23. Paul Gebhardt
24. Jim Lanier
25. Melanie Gould
26. Clinton Warnke
27. Cim Smyth
28. Robert Bundtzen

29. Randy Chappel
30. Lynda Plettner
31. Mike Williams
32. Cali King
33. Cindy Gallea
35. Jack Berry
36. Tyrell Seavey
37. Bill Pinkham
38. Gerald Sousa
39. Carla Kelly
40. Jim Gallea
41. Frank Sihler
42. Kelly LaMarre
43. Ben Stamm
43. Palmer Sagoonick
44. Russell Bybee
SCRATCHED:
Keith Aili
Jason Barron
Peter Bartlett
Lance Barve
Charlie Boulding
Todd Capistrant
Lachlan Clarke
Ted English
Adam Scott Gibler
Ellen Halverson
Bob Hickel
G. B. Jones
Dexter Kancer
Karen Land
Blake Matray
Debbie Moderow
Dean Osmar
Karen Ramstead
Jerry Riley
Perry Solmonson

2004

1. Mitch Seavey
2. Jeff King
3. Kjetil Backen

4. Ramey Smyth
5. Ed Iten
6. Charlie Boulding
7. Rick Swenson
8. Ramy Brooks
9. John Baker
10. Vern Halter
11. Martin Buser
12. Jason Barron
13. Aaron Burmeister
14. Tim Osmar
15. DeeDee Jonrowe
16. Gerald Sousa
17. Ken Anderson
18. Jim Lanier
19. Paul Gebhardt
20. Ray Redington, Jr.
21. Jessie Royer
22. Hugh Neff
23. Melanie Gould
24. Lance Mackey
25. Shannon Brockman
26. Jason Mackey
27. John Barron
28. Fabrizio Lovati
29. Dennis Kananowicz
30. Bill Cotter
31. Nils Hahn
32. Joe Garnie
33. Bill Pinkham
34. Aliy Zirkle
35. Lynda Plettner
36. Sam Perino
37. Mike Williams
38. Robert Bundtzen
39. Frank Sihler
40. William Hanes
41. Cindy Gallea
42. Randy Chappel
43. Cim Smyth
44. Ryan Redington
45. Ellie Claus
46. Rick Mackey

47. Rick Larson
48. Scott Smith
49. Peryll Kyzer
50. Bernard Schuchert
51. Dexter Kancer
52. Noah Burmeister
53. Doug Grilliot
54. Peter Bartlett
55. Kelly Williams
56. Karen Land
57. Rick Casillo
58. Karen Ramstead
59. Al Hardman
60. Ed Stielstra
61. Mark Moderow
62. Tollef Monson
63. Wayne Curtis
64. Russell Bybee
65. Devon Currier
66. Todd Capistrant
67. James Connor
68. Harmony (Kanavale) Barron
69. Cliff Wang
70. Jacob Lysyshyn
71. Matt Weik
72. Sue Allen
73. James Warren
74. Ben Stamm
75. Steve Madsen
76. G. B. Jones
77. Perry Solmonson
SCRATCHED:
Jesse Beebe
Burt Bomhoff
Anna Bondarenko
Todd Denick
Ararad Khatchikian
Sonny Lindner
Judy Merritt
Melinda Miles
Carmen Perzichino

Doug Swingley

2005

1. Robert Sørlie
2. Ed Iten
3. Mitch Seavey
4. Bjornar Andersen
5. Ramy Brooks
6. John Baker
7. Lance Mackey
8. Jessie Royer
9. Paul Gebhardt
10. DeeDee Jonrowe
11. Aliy Zirkle
12. Jeff King
13. Martin Buser
14. Doug Swingley
15. Jessica Hendricks
16. Tyrell Seavey
17. Ken Anderson
18. Hans Gatt
19. Tim Osmar
20. Ramey Smyth
21. Louis Nelson, Sr.
22. Vern Halter
23. Melanie Gould
24. Aaron Burmeister
25. Ray Redington, Jr.
26. Hugh H. Neff
27. Diana (Dronenburg) Moroney
28. Peter Bartlett
29. Harmony (Kanavale) Barron
30. Jason Barron
31. John Barron
32. Gerald Sousa
33. Mark Stamm
34. Cim Smyth
35. Gregg Hickmann
36. Mike Williams
37. Trine Lyrek

38. Sebastian Schnuelle
39. Robert Bundtzen
40. Jim Lanier
41. Michael (Longway) Salvisberg
42. Bill Pinkham
43. Ed Stielstra
44. Judy Currier
45. Aaron Peck
46. Kelley Griffin
47. Bill Steyer
48. Eric Butcher
49. Steve Rasmussen
50. John T. Hessert
51. Dallas Seavey
52. Dodo Perri
53. Bryan Mills
54. Melanie Shirilla
55. Andrew Letzring
56. Debbie Moderow
57. Greg Parvin
58. Tom Knolmayer
59. Jeff Holt
60. Lachlan Clarke
61. Shane Goosen
62. Perry Solmonson
63. Phil Morgan
SCRATCHED:
Charlie Boulding
Bill Cotter
Paul Ellering
Robert Greger
G. B. Jones
Sonny Lindner
Sandy McKee
Gary McKellar
Judy Merritt
Jacques Philip
Karen Ramstead
Rachael Scdoris
Scott Smith
Zack Steer

Rick Swenson
Cliff Wang

2006

1. Jeff King
2. Doug Swingley
3. Paul Gebhardt
4. DeeDee Jonrowe
5. John Baker
6. Bjornar Andersen
7. Ed Iten
8. Jason Barron
9. Mitch Seavey
10. Lance Mackey
11. Jessie Royer
12. Cim Smyth
13. Sonny Lindner
14. Aliy Zirkle
15. Ken Anderson
16. Aaron Burmeister
17. Ramey Smyth
18. Melanie Gould
19. William Hanes
20. Louis Nelson, Sr.
21. Hugh Neff
22. Jacques Philip
23. Martin Buser
24. Jessica Hendricks
25. Mike Jayne
26. Rick Swenson
27. Gerald Sousa
28. Tore Albrigtsen
29. Tove Sørensen
30. Robert Bundtzen
31. Ramy Brooks
32. Bryan Mills
33. Jamie Nelson
34. Rick Casillo
35. Sebastian Schnuelle
36. Hans Gatt
37. Bryan Bearss

38. Fabrizio Lovati
39. Ryan Redington
40. Bill Pinkham
41. Jim Lanier
42. David Sawatzky
43. Christoph Harisberger
44. Tollef Monson
45. Dean J. Rosiar II
46. Ed Stielstra
47. Tom Knolmayer
48. Lynda Plettner
49. Gregg Hickmann
50. Peter Bartlett
51. Paul Ellering
52. Danny Seavey
53. Judy Currier
54. Cindy Gallea
55. Noah Burmeister
56. Tim Osmar
57. Rachael Scdoris
58. Clint Warnke
59. Katie Davis
60. Warren Palfrey
61. Chad Schouweiler
62. Karen Ramstead
63. Lachlan Clarke
64. Ron Cortte
65. Trent Herbst
66. Randy Cummins
67. Kim Kittredge
68. Eric Rogers
69. Katrina Pawlaczyk
70. Steven Madsen
71. Glenn Lockwood
SCRATCHED:
John Barron
Matt Hayashida
Dave Tresino
Terry Adkins
Jim Warren
Richard Hum
Rick Larson

Lori Townsend
Sandy McKee
Sue Morgan
Gary Paulsen
WITHDRAWN:
Ben Valks

Index

Entries in bold type are photographs